13 Feb. 93

To Mike —

May all your dreams
come true —

Much love,
Trey and Melanie

Restaurant Design

Restaurant Design

by Reynaldo Alejandro

PBC INTERNATIONAL, INC.   NEW YORK

Distributor to the book trade in the United States:
Rizzoli International Publications, Inc.
597 Fifth Avenue
New York, NY 10017

Distributor to the art trade in the United States:
Letraset USA
40 Eisenhower Drive
Paramus, NJ 07653

Distributor in Canada:
Letraset Canada Limited
555 Alden Road
Markham, Ontario L3R 3L5, Canada

Distributed throughout the rest of the world by:
Hearst Books International
105 Madison Avenue
New York, NY 10016

Library of Congress Cataloging-in-Publication Data
    Alejandro, Reynaldo G.
    Restaurant Design.
    1. Restaurants, lunch rooms, etc.—United States—
Decoration.   2. Interior decoration—United States—History
—20th century.   I. Title.

NK2195.R4A44   1987   747'.8571'0973   87-61168
ISBN 0-86636-054-9

Color separation, printing, and binding by
Toppan Printing Co. (H.K.) Ltd. Hong Kong

Typesetting by McFarland Graphics Inc.

Printed in Hong Kong
10 9 8 7 6 5 4 3 2 1

Acknowledgements

In the preparation of this book, I am indebted, for their help, support and assistance, to Ivi Cosio Hunter, my research assistant; Cecilia de Castro; Richard Liu; Bing Ruso; Marco Antonio Maltos; Lito Teofisto; Rosemarie De Leon Herbosa; Virginia Christensen; Wanda Jankowski, my editor; and especially to Herb and Cora Taylor, whose foresight and dedication made this book possible.

Publisher	**Herb Taylor**
Project Director	**Cora Sibal Taylor**
Executive Editor	**Virginia Christensen**
Editor	**Wanda P. Jankowski**
Art Director	**Richard Liu**
Production Manager	**Kevin Clark**
Artist	**Donna O'Hare-Patterson**

Contents

Introduction

The atmosphere is as important as the food. This statement would be highly incongruous to the thinking of any other age, but today it is the accepted attitude towards restaurant dining. In an era where space travel and star wars are no longer science fiction, trends in restaurant design have changed at an increasingly faster pace.

Centuries ago, "restaurant" literally meant a place to restore one's energy, or more realistically, a place to be served food and refreshing beverages. The social function of the restaurant—to be a place where people can both meet and see other interesting people—probably developed when the brother of Louis XIII visited a local Paris bistro run by an attractive young woman. Word of the appearance spread throughout the countryside, and the local gentry soon began frequenting the bistro to rub elbows with royalty and to be seen in elegant company.

Then, as today, a restaurant's ambiance reflected the character of its owner, and his or her popularity or status directly influenced the quality of the clientele. In fact, the proprietor's social rank and the quality of the house wine were the two major determinants of the popularity of a restaurant. Hence, to succeed, the restaurateur had to find the right balance between atmosphere and the quality of the food and beverages served.

To the 20th-century diner, ambiance, in combination with good food and service, is still of utmost importance. Consequently, many restaurants that enjoy a reputation for having all these basic elements also have seen the rewards of this successful balance: many years of regular patronage.

But today's metropolises host thousands and thousands of restaurants offering a complete, colorful spectrum of dining couture. Cuisines of all cultures and multitudinous mood-setting decors give unlimited choice to the modern restaurant-goer. The competition has driven restaurateurs to *create* the character and ambiance that in former eras developed slowly through the years. Time is not on the side of the restaurateur—the lifespan of a typical restaurant is only five to seven years.

The contemporary restaurateur must not only elevate his food to an artform but also transform the entire dining process into a well-orchestrated event with the diner in the starring role. All the senses must be satisfied. Bright rooms encourage sociability; darker rooms invite coziness. Noise raises the energy level to produce a highly charged atmosphere while quiet caters to serenity, intimacy, and romance. Thus a restaurant should be designed with a specific set of diners in mind, and attention to detail in matters of ambiance should be given accordingly.

The young urbanite, for example, dines to see as well as to be seen, and lighting plays an important part in the flirtation. He or she wishes not only to look attractive, but also to feel attractive—a goal of design often accomplished through the soft glow of candles on the table or with the discreet, reflected light that bounces off gently painted or textured walls.

The consummate restaurant designer understands the demanding nature of today's clientele and selects carefully every ingredient to lay the basis for an effective combination of practical function and aesthetic enhancement. Everything from the positioning of water stations, to the size of table arrangements, to the type of dinnerware is taken into consideration. Meeting the 20th-century clientele's appetite for change and satisfaction in a material world has heightened the degree of creativity demanded in the field of restaurant design, and the results are exciting.

Fifty recent, innovative designs, employing state-of-the-art materials and techniques and created by the finest restaurant designers in the U.S., have been gathered for presentation in this book. A wide variety of categories is featured, including elegant hotel restaurants and restorations; fast-food, deli, and quick-service eateries; full-service restaurants; clubs and lounges; restaurants specializing in seafood; and nostalgic diners. A range of styles is explored: from formal, opulent ambiance to punk, new-wave influence; from turn-of-the-century Southern refinement to 1950s-inspired collectibility.

Today's designer injects an energy and vibrance into the new artistic milieu of restaurant design, where the platter replaces the palette and the cuisine becomes the canvas. We hope you enjoy this collection of fine and unique dining environments. Bon appetit!

CHAPTER
1

Interviews

Photo: Michael Glover

Hugh Boyd, Carol Hirsch and Martin Dorf

The victorious relocating of Caroline's, a comedy club at New York City's South Street Seaport, was the result of the exceptional collaboration of club owner Carol Hirsch, designer Martin Dorf, and architect Hugh Boyd.

The upscale comedy club was sited in the Chelsea area of the city before moving to its new location—a move that was appropriate as it brought the club closer to the majority of its clientele, employees of the nearby financial district. Unlike most comedy clubs, however, Caroline's did not adopt the basement-level, impoverished look. Instead, the owner opted for a classier reflection of style in decor and appointments, which complemented the entertainment. As a rule of thumb, the club will book only those acts that have received television exposure, to insure a good following every night.

Hirsch scouted for a designer that would understand the market and requirements of the club. A tremendous change was involved as well: Hirsch was upgrading her operations to a full-service restaurant.

Martin Dorf had extensive urban planning experience, having worked with the New York City Planning Commission prior to setting up his own offices. He also was one of the architects chosen by Rouse Company, developers of lower Manhattan's South Street Seaport, to help redesign the restored buildings and enclosed retail areas planned for that historic area. Boyd, who was with Rouse Company, teamed up with Dorf during the South Street Seaport project, and together they have successfully designed such popular food service outlets as New York Fries, La Tablita, and Burger Boys From Brooklyn—all within the Seaport area.

Hirsch was confident in the design acumen of both

men, and hired them to develop the space for the market she envisioned.

At the onset of the project, Hirsch and Dorf discovered that they were attuned to each other's sense of style. Both were inclined to strong, simple statements accentuated with a touch of art. This aesthetic agreement made subsequent problems easier to handle as designer, architect, and client were all in the same frame of mind. It also furthered Hirsch's trust in and openness to the suggestions of Dorf and Boyd. "That's what they're there for. I don't want to work with a designer who will ask me what I want. I want them to tell me what will work," Hirsch said. Their relationship, from conceptualization to finishing touches, was one of honest collaboration—Hirsch setting the guidelines: Boyd and Dorf designing and implementing.

The marketing plan drawn up by Dorf and Associates included a dining hall, a comedy club, and a bar/lounge to maximize profit centers. Thus the space, which occupies 10,000 square feet on two floors of the Link Building at Pier 17, contains two large kitchens, a 150-seat full-service restaurant on the second floor, and a bar with a 150-seat outdoor cafe on the first floor. The comedy club and restaurant are separated by a raw bar, a lounge, and an open grill station.

"This is a true grill restaurant," Hirsch said. "It is simple, fun food with Mexican, Indian, and Italian overtones." Cindy Little was hired as food consultant with Susan Feniger and Mary Sue Milliken, owners of the City Restaurant and the Border Grill in Los Angeles, as consulting chefs.

Dorf and Boyd wanted to create space that would not only maximize profits but also encourage a sense of energy and fun among its patrons. He designed the place for interaction. The style is aggressive: materials are characteristically industrial and stark. Glass garage doors give the cafe and lounge an open ambiance. Black and white are the predominant interior colors. The display grill area is dominated by a large oxidized copper hood, and the bar is constructed of epoxy terrazzo on Plexiglas, backlit for a dramatic effect. A mural is on the wall of the upstairs dining room.

Full kitchens, one on each floor, service the restaurant and cafes. Most storage, prep work, and finishing are done on the first floor, but meals for the main restaurant are cooked in the upstairs kitchen. A dumbwaiter connects the two kitchens.

To top it off, Caroline's has flexible sound and lighting systems, making the club a state-of-the-art media center that can accomodate taped or broadcast television shows, corporate meetings, video productions, theater, music, and, of course, comedy.

Brad Elias

There has been a marked increase in the demands of fine dining over the years because restaurant-goers have become more discerning in their dining preferences. That a place is patronized for its food and service is a given, but today there is an added dimension that a restaurant must offer to ensure repeat business. This element is often difficult to define. Yet, whether dining in a post-modern bistro or catching a fast-food meal in a Victorian setting, the customer must be comfortable enough to enjoy his food, and must enjoy it enough to want to come back another time. What is it that brings customers back to a favorite restaurant again and again?

Ambiance.

Ambiance can be an elusive design goal as it often defies conventional standards and usually goes beyond sensory perception. More than the look of a place, ambiance is the "feel" a restaurant offers. This "feel" rarely happens by accident. It is achieved by combining the facilities, the services, and the objectives of the restaurateur in a total design package. It also includes the structure, layout, style, and marketing goals of a restaurant. It is an exacting business, a business that has been mastered by Brad Elias.

Elias is noted for the success of his projects. He designs in various cities for a variety of clients: food chains, independent restaurants, and hotel dining rooms. Whatever the type of food service, Elias can pull together a dining design that turns profits.

A principal and the design director of the Hochheiser–Elias Design Group, Inc., based in New York and Richmond, Elias has guided into prominence a professional company with a marketing approach to interior design. He started in the business fifteen years ago with a degree in engineering and marketing experience from a major packaged foods manufacturer. In the beginning of his career, he was constantly tested as a newcomer to the field, but his technical background gave him the foundation to make his designs viable. "I do not design anything that cannot be built," says Elias. "There were times when I was told something could not be done. I had to say, 'Give me a hammer and *I'll* show you how'."

Over the years he has developed expertise, and now he enjoys the reputation of being a master in the area of restaurant interior design. His philosophy, influenced largely by his marketing years and mulled through observation and hands-on experience, simply put is "Marketing by Design."

First and foremost, Elias listens closely to what a client wants. He then designs to those specifications. "We consider it our role to be a part of the restaurant's marketing mix. Restaurateurs do not hire a designer to aggrandize their egos. They do it to make money. We should do our part to help maximize their profits, and not create a pedestal artistry."

Important factors must be considered in formulating a plan: the target audience, the type of food, the kind of service, the anticipated peak/busy periods, and the price range. If clients cannot pinpoint what they want, Elias asks them to define what they *do not want*. By this process of elimination, he is able to conceive a clearer idea of their needs. In general, restaurateurs are a savvy lot, so they intuitively know what will work best.

It is the designer's job to bring their ideas to the surface.

With the basic data provided by the client, Elias sets to work with his staff of twelve who, like him, are mostly technically oriented. "When we design, we probably over-design at first," he says. It is a system that allows him to prioritize, eventually trimming down to the basic theme, or ambiance, sought by the client. It may be a piece of sculpture or a platform, but something will emerge as the most definitive item in a place. And budget never undermines design; once the theme has been defined, Elias knows where concessions can be made.

Elevating the Big Mac to a level of fine dining may seem incredulous, but this is what Elias accomplished in a design for the McDonald's franchise in Vineland, New

Jersey. The result was both stylish and profitable.

The owner and Elias decided that bringing the people of Vineland and its nearby towns to fast food required an analysis of the intrinsic values of the potential patron. The restaurant was in the middle of a basically upper-middle-class suburban neighborhood, so Elias picked a Victorian motif to reflect both the tastes of the owner, who happens to be an antique collector, and the upscale attributes of those living and working in the area.

Elias broke the 1,400-square-foot, L-shaped dining room into a series of intimate dining spaces, with post-modern architecture updating the Victorian theme. Natural materials, loose seating, and updated colors boosted its trendy style. Accenting included authentic Victorian pieces. An antique dry sink near the service counter,

stained-glass partitions, and plants were tastefully used to enhance the cozy atmosphere. While the seating capacity was lower than that of the average McDonald's franchise, the seats were designed to be more usable. More duo seating units and counter seating encouraged singles and groups of two to leave the larger table arrangements open for bigger parties. The lighting standards set by McDonald's and devised for rapid turnover were met but modified: softened, indirect illumination sources complemented the Victorian theme without compromise.

To make the place vandal-proof, all fixtures and artworks were permanently attached. Tile flooring and walls were top-coated with a protective sheath to facilitate easy cleaning and maintenance. Use of fabric was minimal, and a resin was used on tables and chairs.

This altogether successful blending of fine style and practical design enabled the McDonald's—Vineland franchise to generate its best possible income.

Another case cited by Elias involved the "facelifting" of a prominent hotel restaurant in Washington, D.C., that eventually scored big marginal gains.

Upon arrival at the hotel restaurant, Elias was surprised that his services were called for. What he saw was an exquisite restaurant, still new, that it did not seem to need the slightest rehabilitation. However, upon closer observation he realized why the place was a financial failure. The layout was isolating, having carried formality to the extreme, and the atmosphere was cold, which was totally inappropriate for its location—a convention hotel where people come to socialize.

First of all, the entrance needed restructuring. An enclosed 20-yard corridor had to be traversed just to arrive at the maitre'd station, thereby discouraging walk-in business. Then Elias noted that the bar was tucked away at the far end of the reception area, making it rather inaccessible and intimidating for a cocktail crowd. Adding to the problem, six- to eight-foot-high partitions blocked the view of the hotel lobby and atrium, and overly discreet recessed lighting did nothing to enhance conviviality.

To turn the place around, the partitions were knocked down, visually opening the area into the lobby. The bar was relocated to an up-front position that people could easily walk to from the maitre'd station. Bar seating was increased from 14 to 47, encouraging large parties to spend time with their drinks, and dinner seating was increased by 28 when smaller tables replaced the oversized existing ones. These new tables were pushed closer together to promote congeniality. The carpeted floors were augmented with more modern surfaces such as wood and tile.

The methods used by Elias in reworking the place to attract patrons were much the same as those used by thriving independent restaurants. The bar was made bigger and was brought closer to the entrance, making it inviting instead of intimidating; partitions and other visual barriers were eliminated, opening up the space and creating a "see and be seen" environment; tables were congregated to make a conduit for the energetic pulse of the room. Finally, hand surfaces were added to help raise the noise level of the room, making the restaurant audibly dynamic and alive.

The contemporary trend of restaurant as theater is a concept Elias has been propagating for years. To this end, however, there will never be a distinct Elias style, no stamp on any project that will announce that the undertaking was an "Elias." Each assignment Elias takes on is given a character of its own to maximize its money-making potential—there is no mass production, no uniformity in his work.

As advice to new designers, Brad Elias says, "Restaurants shouldn't necessarily be done in extreme or severe good taste. People want to be entertained. They want things to hapen in restaurants that they wouldn't necessarily want to happen at home. Restaurant dining should be more fantasy, it should be more dramatic."

Sam Lopata

New York City is well known as one of the premier arenas of theatrical dining, and many attribute this to one man: Sam Lopata. Lopata burst into the restaurant design scene in 1975 with the opening of Chez Pascal. An irrepressible Frenchman with relentless energy, Lopata has since designed places like Pig Heaven, an eclectic Chinese restaurant on the east side of Manhattan, and has presided over the face-lifting of the famed classical French restaurant Lutece. In 1979, Sheldon Haseltine hired Lopata to design Joanna, an overscale brasserie in downtown Manhattan, and a distinctive style was set for scores of restaurants.

"I was the right man at the right time in the right place," says Lopata, whose instinct for the sociology of restaurant-going has always been exquisite. It was Lopata who ushered into New York the era of the grand cafe—an

answer to the restaurant-going public's wish for the convivial and noisy. Lopata insists that noise keeps the adrenalin flowing and creates a dynamic dining environment. These, he says, are the places where people flock.

In addition to his work with restaurants, Mr. Lopata also has over 30 nightclub, retail, and corporate projects nationwide to his credit. From the popular Red Parrot and Private Eyes nightclubs of Manhattan, to the Mikasa boutique in Bloomingdale's; and from the United Status Apparel retail outlet stores in New York, New Jersey, Texas, and Florida to the sparkling Be-la Gelato shop on Lower Broadway, Lopata has brought his keen sensibility to bear on the unique character of each individual space.

Born and raised in Paris, Lopata studied design at the renowned Ecole Nationale de Beaux Arts in France.

After leaving college he spent time on a variety

of pursuits, including the design of a restaurant in Paris where he eventually worked as a bartender "because the job was so much fun." Later, he operated with some friends a section of beach in St. Tropez, which involved selling food and renting mattresses and umbrellas to beach-goers. This was to become the first topless beach, in 1968. Lopata came to New York in 1971. Because he seems to ride on the crest of fashion, people have accused Lopata of being faddish. "I'm not trendy," he says. "The design is only part of the package, and if the management fails, the rest falls apart."

For this reason, Lopata designs specifically for his clients. No matter how frequently he is hired, there will never be a Lopata imprint. He designs around the owner, the restaurant and the food. In this sense, he is a matchmaker. It is Lopata's method to carefully select a design that will jive with not only the type of food, ambiance, and clientele expected at the restaurant, but also the personality and style of the restaurateur. This is the basis of his success.

"Knowing about the food is very important," he asserts. "It has to be matched to the atmosphere, the table settings, the lights—everything!"

Lopata takes great pride in his projects and closely supervises them to see that each is built to his specifications. Most important of all, he says, is to "retain flexibility without compromising the integrity of the design." He leaves room for flexibility because he has learned that no matter how well one plans for a project, something always changes. For example, the restaurant could adopt a clientele entirely different from the one originally expected.

Lopata has a knack for designing much more than lovely spaces. His works embody visions of the future. His most recently completed project is Coastal, a relaxed, subdued Upper West Side restaurant. Coastal's walls are covered with maps of the coastal United States, whetting patrons' appetites for travel, while a space-age bar, all of steel, bears the look of a robot.

Home on the Range, a future undertaking, will be markedly energetic. As the name of the place suggests, Texas cuisine will be served. Lopata envisions the place to be as dynamic as the spicy cuisine, and to contribute to this sense of action, there will be loud music.

"We're seeing a definite return to the tradition of neighborhoods and neighborhood restaurants," he says. "People are looking for a place where they can have a dinner costing less than fifty-dollars and still have fun as in the cafes and brasseries of France."

Restaurant as theater: this is what they want in New York, and Sam Lopata is there to design it for them.

Basic to Sam Lopata's style is his ability to incorporate the personality of the restaurateur, along with the type of food, ambience and clientele, into his designs. As a result, Lopata's creations always remain fresh, exciting and diverse. According to Lopata, "noise keeps the adrenalin going," and noise is a notable factor at restaurants Seiyoken and Extra! Extra! featured in this book.

CHAPTER 2

Full Service Restaurants

This is an era in which dining doubles as entertainment and restaurants offer more than quality food and service. Because people want to be entertained when they step out to dine, the ambiance of a dining environment contributes greatly to its success. Be it a classic French restaurant or a trendy specialty place, "atmosphere" often is what diners will come back for.

Some restaurateurs go so far as to be outstandingly different and, in the process, plan the demise of the place, if only to cash in on its faithful clientele during its lifespan. Some purposely keep the design understated and flexible to accept trends as they come and go. Others design along classic lines to eliminate the risk of being outdated.

Lutece and the Russian Tea Room, both in New York City, have been successful for years because the proprietors understand that quiet hospitality is what their clients want. Formality and Old World charm are their hallmarks.

Newer places thrive on noisier, more public spaces. The philosophy is "see and be seen," "hear and be heard." High noise levels contribute to the dynamism in settings where every patron is invited to take part in the tableau being played. Everyone is a player and spectator at the same time.

Whatever personality a restaurateur conceives for his facility, the key to its success is its ability to meet the demands of its target market. Location is a deciding factor. So is the menu and the type of service the place offers. Each of these elements, along with layout and theme, must be integrated into a design that enchances the sense of drama currently sought by restaurant-goers.

All of the restaurants in this chapter successfully blend these elements. Among them are the following establishments.

- The 500-seat Sports Restaurant, which is designed to express architecturally the image of a sports arena, offers an entertainment atmosphere that is enhanced by exposed, rough-textured brick walls and two huge, steel trusses rising 30 feet above the floor.
- The Art Nouveau style in the Willow Tea Room is evident in the period reproduction furnishings, accessories, and Tiffany-inspired sconces. A striking serpentine ceiling cove is bounded by delicately curved iron arches that extend from floor to ceiling.
- The *trompe l'oeil* of Sgarlato's Cafe depicts a street scene reminiscent of byways found on the Italian Riviera. Marble and ceramic tile floor, marble tabletops, plantings, and cafe-style chairs create an outdoor-cafe feeling.
- Starbuck's Cape Cod style is evident in front porch and railing imagery, weathered shingles, and green willow porch furniture. Aeronautic, folk art, and maritime artifacts individualize the look of the restaurant.

MAX AU TRIANGLE

Project Location:	Beverly Hills, California
Client:	Beverly Rodeo Passage
Interior Designer and Architect:	Stanley Felderman, Leason Pomeroy Felderman Associates
General Contractor:	Buckeye Construction
Structural Engineer:	Erkel/Greenfield
Electrical Engineer:	Angeles Electric
Millwork:	Northwestern Showcase
Renderer:	Stanley Felderman
Photographer:	David Glomb

In keeping with the guidelines of the Beverly Hills City Plan to transform alleys to pedestrian thoroughfares, Max Au Triangle was conceptualized as an interior meeting space, or piazza, along one such route.

Located on the first block of Beverly Drive, just north of Wilshire Boulevard in Beverly Hills, California, the renovated space is built upon a structure erected circa 1906. There are three entry points to the place, and Stanley Sherman played the unique elements of each to an advantage.

Interior features of Le Triangle include the temple ruins fantasy and the guilded elevator tower. The temple setting serves as a gathering space and cafe. The two-story tower elevator delivers patrons to the restaurant, "Max," where they will dine under a barrel vault of golden wire mesh. The vault is one of the original architectural elements uncovered during the stripping away of the building's many layers. Elements from other eras of the building's were similarly exposed and incorporated into the design, creating a rich layering of time, image, and material.

The success of the design lies in the juxtapositioning of hard and soft, formal and informal, and oblique and straight angled elements.

A fantasy version of an inverted temple sits in the piazza-like interior.

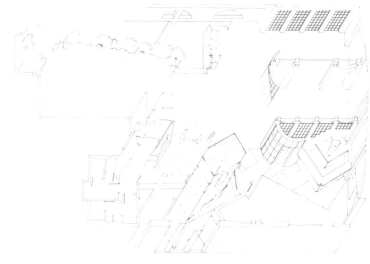

The ceiling grid belongs to the original 1906 structure. It was discovered when layers of renovated structure were peeled away.

AURORA

Project Location:	New York, New York
Client:	Joe Baum
Interior Designers:	Milton Glaser (*principal*), Tim Higgins (*project designer*), Milton Glaser, Inc.
Associate Interior Designer:	The Office of Philip George
Architect:	Tim Higgins, Milton Glaser, Inc.
Lighting Designer:	Paul Marantz, Jules Fisher & Paul Marantz, Inc.
Mechanical and Electrical Engineers:	Robins Engineering
Bar Sculpture:	Jordan Steckel
Photographer:	Jon Naar, Jon Naar Photography

Months before Aurora opened, the Manhattan restaurant scene was abuzz, with speculation on this latest design venture of food-service industry maven Joseph Baum. Baum is responsible for such restaurant design classics as Windows on the World and The Four Seasons, but he had definite ideas for Aurora, his own restaurant. He wanted superb food in a comfortable environment where the serious executive could have a satisfying lunch and the light-hearted pleasure seeker could find the ideal evening. He wanted a facility where both men and women would be comfortable to dine and entertain. The result is an elegant, warm place—clublike during lunch, romantic in the evening.

Aurora cannot be called a trendy restaurant. Its design is based on the classic guidelines of comfort and fine cuisine. It is a place where patrons find both satisfaction and intrigue. These are the timeless qualities that bring back Aurora's clientele time and time again.

Curved and rounded forms dominate the restaurant space, in the lighting fixtures, bar rail, tile–carpet edges, and seating coves.

Emerging faces and circles contribute to the unique, off-beat styling of the restaurant.

The bar area is dominated by lighting-fixture bowls of pastel-colored cast plastic.

The low ceiling is made to seem higher than it is through the uplighting of a cove built into a wood valance. A soft glow emanates from the delicate glass wall sconces.

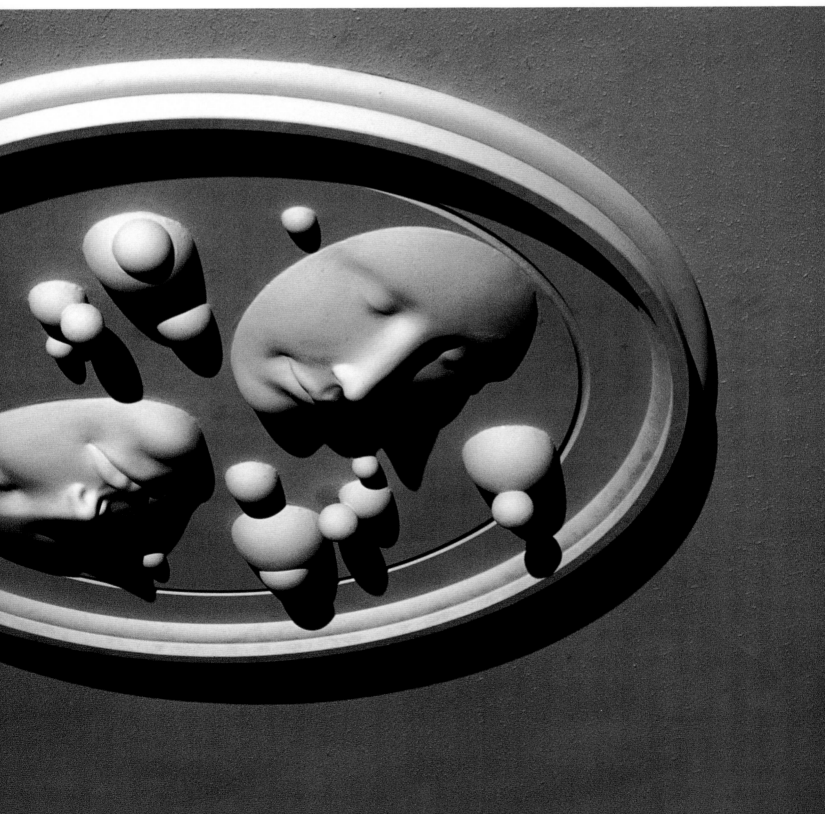

The polished granite bar is designed to be the centerpiece of the room—a dining area at lunchtime and a gathering place in the evening.

The setting is designed to appeal to both men and women. The room takes on a club-like feeling at lunchtime.

UNION SQUARE CAFE

Project Location:	New York, New York
Owner:	Daniel Meyer
Interior Designer and Architect:	Larry Bogdanow, R.A. Warren Ashworth (*project manager*), L. Bogdanow & Associates, Architects
Lighting Designer:	Celeste Gainer, Gotham Light & Power
General Contractor:	David Elliot Construction
HVAC:	Kayback
Graphic Artist:	Andrea DaRiff
Artists:	Judy Rifka, Susan Walp, Jim Gingerich
Photographer:	Daniel Eifert

The 4,000 square foot Union Square Cafe is divided into three areas: the bar, the main dining room and the rear Garden Dining Room. The interior walls are cream-colored with dark-green painted wainscoting. Paintings placed throughout the restaurant provide the main decorative features. The styles of the paintings range from neo-impressionist to naive and most are still lifes of food. Ceiling heights have been raised to maximum levels, and vary throughout the cafe.

The 65-seat stepped-down main dining area is entered from the bar and receives soft illumination from a bank of windows facing the street. Cherrywood flooring extends the cozy atmosphere.

The 45-seat Garden Dining Room at the rear is named for the small tree-and-flower planted outdoor corridor beyond the cafe's windows. The 20-foot ceiling allows for a 21-seat balcony that overlooks the main dining space.

◁ The mural by Judy Rifka was commissioned by the owner. The mezzanine office has been converted into a balcony dining area.

A sense of warmth is created in the bar area with wooden beams, mahogany bar, terra-cotta floor tile, and beam-recessed lighting units fitted with warm-colored filters.

CAFE SEIYOKEN

Project Location: New York, New York
Client: Tony Tokunaga
Interior Designer: Sam Lopata, Sam Lopata Inc.
Lighting Designer: Ken Billington, Ken Billington, Inc.
Photographer: Norman McGrath

Cafe Seiyoken offers a Japanese/French menu and reflects this unusual combination in its layout and design. The seating for 200 in the large, bright dining room is clustered around the columns, and is reminiscent of a Parisian brasserie. A classic Japanese, grid-like motif is carried through the cafe—in the mirrored walls, and in the three-tiered light fixtures at the tops of the black-painted structural columns.

A madrone wall moulding directly above the banquettes matches the ceiling moulding. Custom-designed chairs covered with bold zebra stripes add energy to the black and white palette of the interior. Exotic floral arrangements are displayed in sleek black granite cabinets.

Acoustic control is kept at a minimum because noise is considered a positive factor. Light levels are bright enough to illuminate the fashion and show business clientele who come to see and be seen, as much as to enjoy the food and service. The column light fixtures combine fluorescent and incandescent units, and are augmented by overhead framing projectors and round incandescent wall fixtures.

Zebra stripes on chairs energize the black and white color scheme.

CADILLAC GRILLE

Project Location:	Jackson, Wyoming
Owners and Design Team Leaders:	Ken and Suzanne Rominger, Rom Corporation
Interior and Lighting Designer:	Harold E. Tubbs, A.S.I.D., Contract Design
Architect:	Danny Williams, A.I.A., Atelier One Ltd.
Contractor:	Mark Klinzman Construction
Photographers:	Mark Rohde (*interiors*), Ed Riddell (*exteriors*)

The Cadillac Grille in Jackson, Wyoming, offers its clientele relief from the cowboy atmosphere and western music common to restaurants of the area. It is the only Art Deco restaurant in town; consequently, it enjoys tremendous popularity and patronage.

The owners of the Cadillac Grille served as the restaurant's design team leaders, for both were well versed in the style and details of the period. They knew exactly what their ideas required and had an excellent vision of the end product. They started by dividing the original space into three separate rooms to segregate the secluded, quiet areas from those intended for more social dining.

The main dining room, with its flexible table groupings and small booth along the perimeter, encourages conviviality, while the other, smaller room, with its built-in booth arrangement, offers tranquil, intimate seating. Marble floorings and other glossy, sound-reflecting surfaces in the bar area amplify the noise, contributing to the level of energy and activity in the restaurant.

Marble and glass blocks lend a touch of elegance and add contrast to the darker shades of the main dining room.

The custom-designed bar is highlighted by etched glass in an underlit countertop.

A quiet area behind the bar is furnished with high-backed, built-in booths. The pastel-colored stepped ceiling softens the space.

Illumination from under the lip of the bar contrasts with the dark countertop. The bar stools are designed in sleek Deco style.

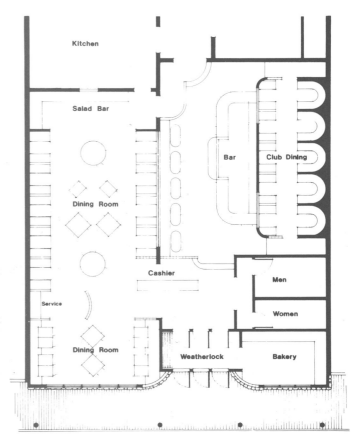

Soft, pastel lighting flatters the complexion. Deco themes are extended into the ceiling.

EXTRA! EXTRA!

Project Location: New York, New York
Client: Extra, Extra restaurant
Interior Designers: Sam Lopata, Denise Hall
Lighting Designer: Ken Billington
Photographer: Milroy/McAleer Photography

Extra! Extra! opened in 1986 with a conservative, subdued interior. Six months later, the restaurant closed for two weeks and reopened as the new, transformed Extra! Extra!

The designer used the restaurant's name and location (the first floor of the *Daily News* building) as the basis for introducing a pop art newspaper theme. Larger than life plywood cutouts of popular cartoon characters, such as Blondie, Dagwood, Felix the Cat, and Dick Tracy are scattered throughout the 160-seat restaurant. The black-and-white color scheme with red accents, large personal ads behind the bar, crossword puzzles, sports and real estate listings, and ink spots splattered on the floor reinforce this theme.

Overhead, a suspended black grid sits under a bare concrete ceiling with exposed mechanical ductwork. Bare, low wattage incandescent lighting is used, as well as ceiling-mounted can lights, which are angled to shine on cartoon-theme hanging lamps that add to the tongue-in-cheek design.

The restaurant is divided into three dining areas and has a centrally located 25-seat bar, to encourage friendly conversation among patrons. Sixties music is played to enhance the familiar and informal atmosphere of the restaurant as well as to promote a nostalgic feeling.

Cartoon character, Wimpy, greets customers near the entrance wearing a chef's hat and apron. The old tile floor is splattered with newspaper ink blots.

A metal grid is suspended over the bare concrete ceiling. Bare, low-wattage incandescent bulbs, with sparkling filaments, are attached to old-fashioned, black and white cords and draped through the metal grid.

L'ERMITAGE

Project Location: Los Angeles, California
Client: Dora Fourcade
Interior and Lighting Designer, and Architect: Michael Payne, A.S.I.D., Michael Payne Design
Photographer: Phillip Nilsson, Phillip Nilsson Photography

The redesign of L'Ermitage presented two major challenges. First, the landmark Los Angeles restaurant needed to update its look while maintaining an elegance consistent with its stature. Second, the original layout of the restaurant had made it necessary to seat many guests in a series of rooms towards the back; the space needed restructuring to make all areas of the restaurant bright and inviting.

The entry is relocated at the center, and guests may now choose the front room for its fireplace, the entry room for its buffet and open seating, or the back room for its glass-domed patio fountain. The new design also allows for the opening of doors and windows to create the larger space needed to accommodate large parties. Classical columns in the dining area and entry further emphasize the timeless grace of the restaurant. In the patio and elsewhere, stone mouldings continue this theme.

The successful combination of open design, light colors, natural materials, and classical elements, make L'Ermitage a modern statement of traditional beauty.

The blond-colored chairs, cabinets, and bar reflect a feeling of lightness and openness appropriate to the sunny California location.

INDIAN OVEN II

Project Location:	New York, New York
Client:	Indian Oven Restaurants, Inc.
Interior and Lighting Designer, and Architect:	Steven K. Peterson, and Barbara Littenberg, Peterson, Littenberg, Architects
Contractor:	Mayo Construction Co.
Engineer:	Bong Yu, P.C.
Photographer:	Peter Margonelli

"We set out to make an architecturally good environment for eating, rather than a restaurant with interior decoration," claims Steven K. Peterson who with Barbara Littenberg designed the Indian Oven. They created a "modern space" instead of a decorated dining place.

Arches are used throughout the long and narrow space, to solve the problem of progression. This device serves as a design similar to thresholds and gateways characteristic of Indian Mogul Gardens. The trim that appears on the facade is repeated in reduced scale throughout the interior providing continuity and animation; volume is established by connecting walls, ceilings, and floors. The harmony created by the subtle use of classic architectural motifs and clean contemporary design results in a pristine look. By conceptualizing a metaphoric garden with linked arcades, Peterson and Littenberg convey the essence of Islamic architecture to reflect the restaurant's cuisine without having to deal with a pastiche of Indian objects.

The 100-seat restaurant is 100 feet long and 12 feet wide. In addition to the bar and main dining area, it includes a kitchen, office, and basement party room.

Mirrors allow the space to appear larger than it really is. Though the client did not wish ornate, traditional Indian elements to dominate the space, the coves and varied, angled planes create a refreshing garden feeling.

AMERICA

Project Location: New York, New York

Client: Yvette Durant, Ark Restaurant Corp.

Interior Designer and Architect: McClintock Grammenopoulos Soloway (MGS) Architects

Lighting Designer: Consolidated Edification

Photographer: Masao Ueda

The fresh, exciting style of America is established at the entrance. On the exterior, the name "America" is inlaid in brass in the concrete step, a sandblasted star sits atop a 10-foot brass pole, and nine 11-inch white neon stars are scattered over the facade. The restaurant is 2 feet, 6 inches above the street level. The glass line is set 8 inches behind the existing cast iron mullion to accentuate the height of the masonry opening, and unify the facade by leaving an unglazed plane of cast iron columns and mullions across both windowed and open porch bays. The lighted back wall of the restaurant is visible from the street.

Oblique angles are used throughout the interior to stimulate visually by delaying spatial comprehension. The entry is angled covered porch and vestibule. Overhead, the blue ceiling is pierced by star-like low-voltage downlights laid out in the configuration of the night sky on July 4, 1776.

Interior furnishings include round oak tables and oak school chairs. Side platforms covered with black and white tile support tables and swivel chairs. Strips of colored neon representing the U.S. flag are ceiling mounted and extend over the aisle to the bar. Stars are projected on an angled path from ceiling-suspended theatrical lighting fixtures. Black columns and masonry sandblasted piers are scattered throughout the large, high-ceilinged room.

Wooden school chairs in the center of the room and swivel chairs on the black-and-white tiled, raised side platforms contribute to the informal atmosphere.

Interest in the space is created through extensive use of oblique angles—in the neon stripes of the flag, the wall murals, and the aisle.

The murals, reminiscent of fragments of Navajo sandpainting, depict a variety of American scenes.

WILLOW TEA ROOM

Project Location: Carmel, California
Clients: Joan and Don Miller
Interior Designer: Michelle Pheasant, I.B.D., and Linda S. Lamb, I.B.D., Michelle Pheasant Design, Inc.
Architect: G. D. Case, Case Associates, Architecture
Lighting Designer: Donald Maxcy, Design Associates
Murals: Paul Willner
Photographer: Russell Abraham, Russell Abraham Photography

The Willow Tea Room is the result of its owners' passion for Art Nouveau objects: the restaurant design showcases and regales the romantic era of the 1900s. Located in Carmel, California, mini-mall, the restaurant occupies 4,800 square feet of boxlike space with two existing columns that originally presented a design problem. These "obstacles," however, have been converted into the restaurant's focal point—a curved arc of iron fretwork that adorns the ceiling—which now serves as a thematic agent throughout the restaurant.

The 1900s ambience of the restaurant is established at the entrance, where striking bronze nymph greets guests upon their arrival. The period reproduction chairs, the rich fabrics, the deep wood tones, and the low lighting levels all contribute to the enchanting ambiance. Color selections are elegant grey-green, peachy pink, apricot, and plum. A uniformity in the recessed, colored lighting units is offset by the sparkle of Tiffany-inspired sconces in lily-shaped forms.

© Russell Abraham 1986

Iron fretwork formed into sinuous arches borders the glowing serpentine cove overhead and continues to wind through other portions of the restaurant. A typically Nouveau peacock motif is printed on the linen chair coverings.

The Cranston Room, a private dining area, is furnished with restored Art Nouveau furniture and accessories. The hand-painted frieze depicting peacocks is by artist Paul Willner.

Rich furnishings help to create the refined, elegant, relaxed dining atmosphere reminiscent of a bygone era.

© Russell Abraham 1986

© Russell Abraham 1986

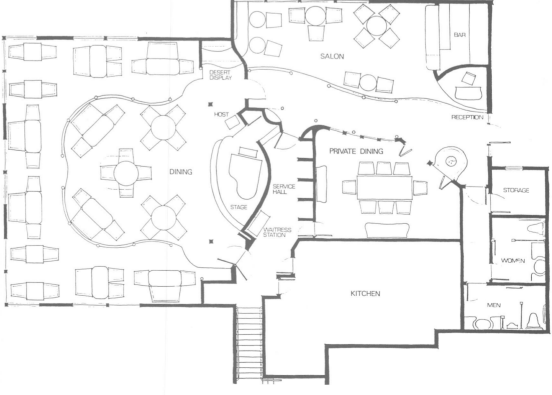

An Art Nouveau chandelier from the client's collection is suspended in the center of the oblong skylight, which is positioned in the center of the dining room. The interplay of curvilinear shapes adds interest to the space.

A harsh amount of daylight was eliminated by closing off four of the existing 16 windows. The recessed spots and downlights are fitted with plum-colored filters.

© Russell Abraham 1986

STARBUCK'S

Project Location: Hyannis, Massachusetts
Client: 518 Realty Corporation
Interior Designers: Blase Gallo, Peter Niemitz, Morris Nathanson, (*project designers*), Morris Nathanson Design, Inc.
Photographer: Warren Jagger

Hyannis, Massachusetts, is attracting an ever-increasing number of young people, both tourists and residents. This popularity has created a year-round market where expendable income is attracted to the fun of exciting, sophisticated restaurants and nightclubs. Starbuck's is designed to appeal to this market.

Since the building is adjacent to the Hyannis airport, aeronautic imagery abounds. An extensive array of historical airplane prints was donated by the owners from their personal collections, and "Starbuck," an old Cape Cod/Nantucket area name, was selected by the designers to represent the mannequin navigator who sits in the genuine World War II Fokker airplane hanging from the rafters. Whimsical artifacts,

Porch railing is used throughout the restaurant. Liquor is displayed in hanging bird feeders.

At the back bar, a large open house
distinguished by four Georgian pillars,
is capped by a cupola and a buggy
weather vane.

Whimsical artifacts indigenous to the area, such as antique framed photos, and maritime and folk art objects, are placed throughout the restaurant and encourage a lighthearted atmosphere.

The lower dining level is enhanced by wicker furniture. The wood is pickled in some areas with white stain.

The restaurant is named after the famed navigator, who is represented by the mannequin seated in the genuine World War 2 Fokker airplane suspended from the rafters.

BLOOMSBURY

Project Location: New York, New York
Client: Carl Butera
Architect: Martin E. Dorf, Dorf Associates
Lighting Designer: Carroll Cline, Cline, Bettridge, Bernstein
Graphic Artist: Tom Gould
Photographer: Mark DeSimone

In designing Bloomsbury, on New York City's Third Avenue, the designer faced the challenge of creating a warm, inviting restaurant that would attract an upscale crowd from the surrounding neighborhood. Complicating the task was the long, narrow existing space, which had previously housed several unsuccessful restaurants.

The designers chose to draw upon the ambiance, design, and materials of an historic district adjacent to the restaurant. This had the desired effect of linking Bloomsbury to the neighborhood and making it an integral part of the area. The use of Victorian details similar to those in the historic district, including brass railings, wood paneling, brick, and glass blocks, warms the otherwise contemporary atmosphere of the restaurant.

The 2,000 square-foot restaurant in midtown Manhattan comprises four areas: a dining area on the lower level, an espresso bar, the bar, and a dining area on the upper level. Varied ceiling heights and floor levels help separate the areas, and a large stainless steel duct runs the length of the restaurant, separating the bar and the adjacent dining area.

Solar bronze windows running from floor to ceiling face the street and reveal an attractive and welcoming place. Glass block, used to separate the kitchen from one of the dining areas and elsewhere in the restaurant, helps give an open feeling to the 22-foot-wide space.

The overscaled, stainless-steel duct that runs through the restaurant houses the HVAC. The long brass rail that separates the bar from the dining area is supported by stainless-steel cable anchored in the overhead duct.

The bar is placed adjacent to the dining area to allow patrons to see and be seen, and to promote steady turnover at lunchtime.

PALIO

Location: New York, New York
Interior Designer and Architect: Raul de Armas (*design partner*),
Thomas Fridstein (*partner-in-charge*),
Skidmore, Owings & Merrill
Lighting Designer: Jules Fisher and Paul Marantz Inc.
Graphics and Tableware Design: Vignelli Associates
Photographer: Wolfgang Hoyt, ESTO
Photographics

The two-story Palio restaurant and bar is located in the Equitable Center in New York City. The 54-foot by 124-foot ground-level room is paneled with rich European bog oak and contains a bar made of one, large, uncut piece of dark Roncevalles marble with a honed finish. The bar is set above chrome-framed, stainless-steel mesh panels, where the spats of the bar chairs and the staccato pattern of the Bianco di Nieve and Belgian black marble floor lend unity to similar motifs found in the Neo-Expressionist mural mounted over the dado. The spectacular, colorful mural depicts the medieval race for which the restaurant is named.

The second-floor dining room is reached by private elevator and seats 120. Two additional private dining rooms seat 40. The dining room is distinguished by delicately patterned wooden screens, translucent honey-onyx panels, and Andover chairs. These elements provide a sedate and elegant setting for the decorative Vignelli designs, which are included in the linen, flatware, silver, menus, dishes, coatracks, and even the waiters' uniforms. Heraldic symbols, which represent the 17 contrade, or wards, of the City of Siena, adorn the walls and embellish colorfully the golden table settings.

Patterned wooden screens and translucent honey-onyx panels adorn the dining room.

The bar is made from a slab of dark Roncevalles marble. The bar-area walls are paneled with European bog oak.

The neo-expressionist mural above the bar, by Sandro Chia, depicts the medieval race after which the restaurant is named.

◊ *The 120-seat dining room is reached by private elevator.*

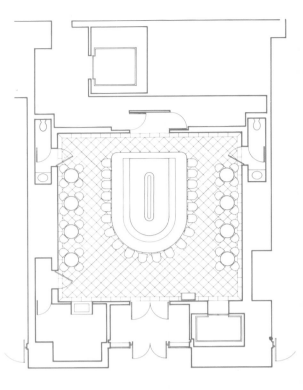

Golden table settings bear heraldic symbols representing the 17 contrade, or wards, of the City of Siena.

THE ASSEMBLY

Project Location: Manalapan, Florida
Client: Jerry Ossip
Interior and Lighting Designer: Brad Elias, Hochheiser-Elias Design Group, Inc.
Photographer: Peter Paige, Peter Paige Associates

An offshoot of the owner's New York Assembly Steakhouse, the Assembly Restaurant attracts many of the same customers on their winter vacations. The owner therefore required that there be a continuity of typical Steakhouse elements, such as wood and beveled or etched glass, and that the creation relay to customers an overall feeling of timelessness. Thus the restaurant could not be trendy, post-modern, or Art Deco. The target patron of this restaurant was sophisticated but not avant-garde, in a high income bracket, and appreciative of a fine meal in a comfortable, interesting, unpretentious environment.

Within the confines of the owner's aesthetic criteria, the designer also has integrated humorous, offbeat touches that add another dimension to the restaurant—imitation, slightly bawdy antiques and black-and-white artwork of whimsical themes, respectively positioned and framed in mock-formal manner.

The timeless decor evident at the grand stair uses elements found in other branches of the steakhouse chain—rich wood, beveled and etched glass, individually lighted steps.

On the lower level, the piano lounge overlooks the dining platform.

On the upper level, patrons can enjoy
a full continental menu in a
comfortable library-like setting.

The skylight and 16-foot Ficus tree in ▷
the pub-like bar area provide visual
interest for balcony diners.

SPORTS RESTAURANT

Project Location: New York, New York

Client: Donald S. Reiter

Interior and Lighting Designers and Architects: Patricia Sapinsley (*principal*), Deborah Heffter, Chris Kauffmann, Paul Gallagher, Margaret Leporati (*assistants*), Patricia Sapinsley Architecture

Photographer: Ken Katz

The space that houses the 500-seat, 6,000-square-foot Sports Restaurant formerly had been occupied by a supermarket, and originally had been a movie theater. Extensive renovation of the building was required to accommodate the new restaurant, including the addition of two floors.

The restaurant's sports atmosphere is not created through the typical technique of randomly placed sports memorabilia. The sports image is conveyed, instead, mainly through the architecture, which is designed to resemble a small stadium. After stripping the interior during the renovation of the space, two huge, riveted, trusses, 30 feet above the floor, and rough structural bricks were uncovered. These served as the inspiration for the architect's concept because they suggested the structure and tough character of a sports stadium.

The architect studied sports arenas, particularly the structures of the Harvard, Brown, and Cornell stadiums, and the Roman Coliseum. Steel beams and brick have been left exposed. Sporting events can be viewed by patrons on three giant video screens and on numerous smaller television screens from tables, a double row of bleachers, or the long bar.

Sports fans can view events on three giant video screens, or on the smaller television screens scattered throughout the restaurant.

There is no superficial sports memorabilia cluttering the walls. The stadium theme is embodied in the architecture.

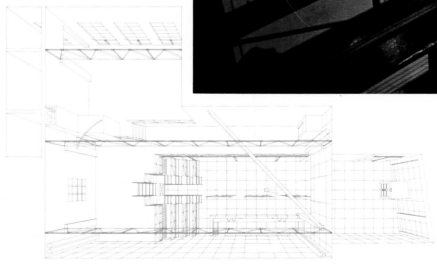

Sports seats 500. Structural steel trusses beneath the 30-foot-high ceiling are left exposed.

THE BALLROOM

Project Location: New York, New York
Client: Felipe Roja Lombardi
Interior and Lighting Designer: Jack Ceglic
Architect: Ervin Lemberger, Lemberger Brody Assoc.
Artist: Marian Pinto (*interior and exterior murals*)
Photographer: Harold Naideau, Naideau Studios

The Ballroom's tapas bar, dining room and cabaret are located on one floor and are designed to operate independently. A cornucopia of colorful foods is displayed on an oversized mahogany bar reminiscent of those used in the Prohibition Era, and is hung from a rack over the bar. Customers can view and choose game to be used for their next day's dinner.

The crisp, clean atmosphere of a bistro is projected through the use of white: white draperies at the windows, and tables covered with white tablecloths and white butcher paper. The tile floors extend the clean image and complement the shiny, cream walls.

Pastries and cheeses are displayed on butcher blocks in the dining area. In the lounge, a butcher block floor serves as a stage or as a serving table. Though The Ballroom serves year-round staples, the decor and many menu items change seasonally.

Kitchen-style elements are used in the dining area, such as the butcher block tables on which the pastries are displayed.

Beige and green floor tile, and white tablecloths covered with white butcher paper create a clean, crisp look.

Game is suspended above the tapas bar, and can be viewed and reserved by customers for next day dinners. A bounty of year round and seasonal foods adorns the bar.

CHAPTER
3

Hotel Restaurants

The histories of the food service and hospitality industries go hand in hand. In bygone eras, it was customary for small inns to charge guests for both room and repast, whether or not the food was eaten. Entire meals were served on long tables at fixed hours, and guests helped themselves.

With the advent of luxury hotels, this practice was largely replaced. *Table d'hote* meals in courses were first offered by The Tremont House in Boston in the 1830's. These meals were elaborately presented by waiters who were drilled to serve each course with military precision. Other hotels soon adopted the practice, and dining at hotel restaurants became a memorable experience. In time, luxurious dining was strongly identified with hotels. Independent restaurants could only copy and hope to equal the food and service that the hotels offered.

Today, hotel restaurants compete with the full-service restaurants in every city. While the independent restaurant has the versatility to respond immediately to trends, most hotel dining places are saddled with the problem of attracting local customers and in-house guests. Major hotels usually try to offer a variety of food services, so one commonly finds a coffee shop, a bar/cocktail lounge, and a formal dining facility in these places.

The key to successful hotel dining is the food and service, and the designer must work closely with the food and beverage manager. One major consideration is seating. A mixture of banquettes and chairs is highly recommended; long banquettes and armless chairs should be avoided. In general, the designer should keep in mind that a logical design is what works best in hotel food outlets.

Several styles are represented in this chapter. A traditional, English pub atmosphere is carried through the bar and dining room at The Canterbury Hotel via rich elements such as upholstered mahogany furniture and wall-mounted duck prints. The interiors of the American Harvest Restaurant at the Vista International Hotel are reminiscent of an 18th-century Federal townhouse: each of the five dining rooms is distinguished by a different color scheme, and the rooms are separated by glass vitrines containing American arts and crafts exhibits. An elegant grandeur is conveyed in the French Room at The Adolphus Hotel with a design modeled after the 18th-century palaces and chateaus of Europe: the vaulted ceiling and columned walls are adorned with rococo murals by noted scenic artists. The revamped Americus Restaurant uses brass, panels of chrome, and glass to create an entirely contemporary environment where gracefully arched glass tree lights add sparkle and dimension. Chez Antoine's three distinct eating and drinking areas—the greenhouse cafe/lounge, the bar, and the more formal dining room—are united by the sumptuous materials and elegant details used throughout: heavy brocade and tapestry fabrics, fringed lamp shades, custom-made tiles and light fixtures, and beveled mirrors.

THE CANTERBURY HOTEL RESTAURANT

Project Location:	Indianapolis, Indiana
Client:	The Canterbury Hotel
Interior Designers:	Peter Niemitz, Blase Gallo, Morris Nathanson, (*project designers*), Morris Nathanson Design, Inc.
Architect:	James Jalliffe, Browning, Day, Mullins & Dierdorf
Photographer:	Gregory Murphy

The 1910 timeworn building which now houses The Canterbury Hotel had lacked a cohesive architectural style. Interior architecture combined Greek revival, Moroccan, Moorish, Incan rococo, Art Deco and moderne influences.

The building has been rehabilitated and restored to reflect a luxury hotel image. Approximately 25 percent of the original architectural features have been retained to comply with tax benefit regulations. Original details are painted white to unify the mixed architectural styles.

The ground floor bar and restaurant are accessed through the hotel's entry vestibule. A club-like atmosphere is projected in both the bar and the adjacent restaurant through details such as wall-mounted artworks, and rich, mahogany paneling and millwork. At midday, lunches are served in the informal bar area, which features traditional upholstered furniture and an array of duck prints. Daylight filters in through Belgian-lace curtained windows. The more formal, 40-seat restaurant offers three meals a day.

Warm colors and traditional furniture induce a feeling of comfort in a private dining area.

Warm colors and traditional furniture induce a feeling of comfort in a private dining area.

Mahogany paneling and millwork add richness and warmth to the 40-seat restaurant.

Traditional-styled upholstered furniture and wall-mounted duck prints create a club-like atmosphere in the bar.

AMERICAN
HARVEST
RESTAURANT
Vista International Hotel

Project Location:	New York, New York
Client:	Vista International Hotel
Interior Designer and Architect:	Leon Moed (*partner in charge*), Donald C. Smith (*design partner*), Manuel Fernandez, Richard Allen, Peter H. Brown, Doug Johnson, Donald Sullivan (*design team*), Davis Allen, Carrell Murphy, Vincent Nealy (*interior design*)
Interior Design Consultant:	David T. Williams, Inc.
Lighting Designer:	Wheel Gersztoff Friedman Associates, Inc.
General Contractor:	Morse Diesel Inc.
Engineers:	Weiskopf & Pickworth; Jaros, Baum & Bolles
Photographer:	Wolfgang Hoyt, ESTO Photographics

American Harvest is the showcase restaurant of the Vista International Hotel at the World Trade Center in New York City. As the name suggests, it offers home-grown all-American cuisine.

To complement the culinary theme, the interior is reminiscent of an 18th-century Federal townhouse. Located at the southern end of the plaza level of the hotel, the irregularly shaped space was converted to five rooms, four devoted to intimate dining.

Each of the four dining areas has its own color scheme: blue, peach, coral, green.

Ficus trees decorated with sparkling lights are housed in five large, round planters which encircle the buffet counter.

Etched and backlighted bronze mirrored-glass mural panels above the Tall Ships Bar depict scenes of tall ships in New York Harbor in the 19th century.

The Greenhouse Restaurant is housed in an enclosed two-story glass structure. The color scheme is soothing and relaxing, using pinks, moss green, and jade.

THE FRENCH ROOM
ADOLPHUS HOTEL

Project Location:	Dallas, Texas
Client:	Westgroup, Inc. of Los Angeles, and the New England Mutual Life Insurance Company
Interior and Lighting Designers:	Jill Kurtin-Cole and Rikki Dallow, Swimmer Cole Martinez Curtis
Architect:	Overton Shelmire, Beran-Shelmire Architects
Ceiling Murals:	James L. Fraser (*designer*), Peter Wolf, James Finger (*team leader*)

The most important design objective for The French Room, as well as for the entire Adolphus project, was to create a hotel as grand and glamorous as the one conjured by nostalgic memory. For when actual photographs of the old hotel were shown to the people who remembered its best years, the real picture did not approach the magnificence of the reminiscence. The designer set out to make manifest the hotel of everyone's fantasy.

There were no significant structural limitations encountered in the redesign of The French Room. However, due to the historical status of the space, the basic structural elements could not be changed or demolished. The French Room was one of the few spaces in the hotel that had remained basically the same over the years, but the integrity of its original design—cold, white plaster walls, gold-veined mirrored tiles, boarded-up windows, and red velvet drapes—had been lost to time. The designer recaptured that integrity with an entirely new interior.

The walls and ceiling are adorned with murals of La Belle Epoque, complete with cherubs, ribbons, clouds, and trompe l'oeil landscapes. The one-piece carpet is 30 by 70 feet.

Before renovation, the bottleneck entrance, the positioning of the bar in a far corner, and the harsh lines of the decor made the restaurant unappealing to conventioneers staying at the hotel.

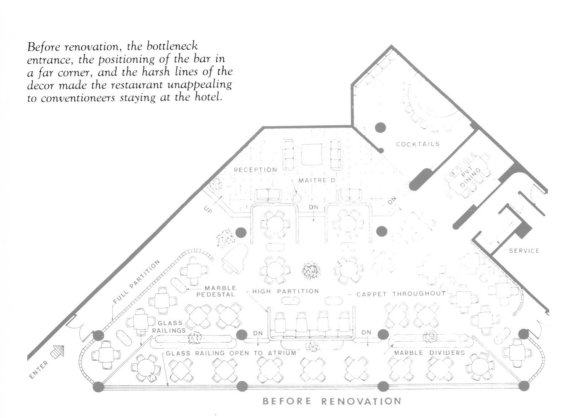

BEFORE RENOVATION

An oyster bar, wine display, and piano-bar lounge have been added to the restaurant. Seating is distributed on multi-level platforms.

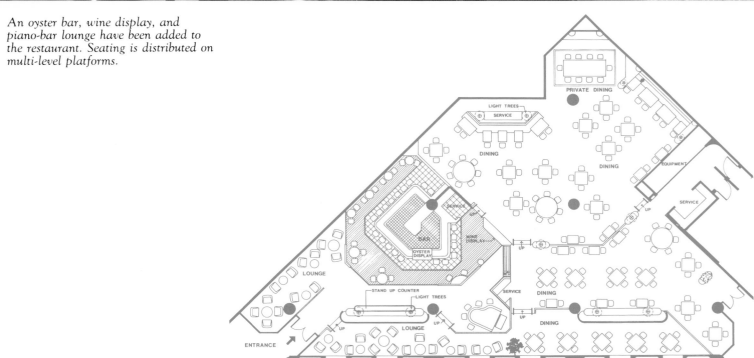

AFTER RENOVATION

The bar was moved from a back corner to the front of the restaurant for the convenience of single diners—food is served at the bar counter—and for those who wish to forgo dinner and stop by for a drink only. Seating in the bar/lounge has been increased from 14 to 47.

A secluded corner for small, private parties is included. The rose tortoise-glass light fixtures add soft, flattering illumination to the space.

CHEZ ANTOINE
LE GRAND HOTEL

Project Location: Montreal, Canada
Client: Hotels of Distinction, Incorporated
Interior Designers: Peter Niemitz, Blase Gallo, Morris Nathanson, Norman Latour, (*project designers*), Morris Nathanson Design, Inc.
Architect: Pauline Barrable, David, Boulva, Cleve
Photographer: Warren Jagger

Chez Antoine's French Epoque style reflects its new European-style ownership and management.

Le Grand Hotel's food service needs are met by the three separate and distinct dining areas of Chez Antoine. The greenhouse cafe/lounge offers light meals and includes a bar which serves as a casual meeting place. The large main dining room can be used for any occasion. The quiet, more subdued dining area is appropriate for small groups and more formal dining.

A diversity of select materials are used throughout Chez Antoine to carry out the functional and aesthetic objectives of the design. These include Parisian metro wall tiles, patterned terrazzo flooring, highly reflective painted surfaces, curved mouldings, deep-coffered ceilings, quilt railings, ornate metalwork, heavily brocaded fabrics, tapestries, fringed lamp shades, a melange of hand-painted tiles, custom light fixtures, and beveled mirrors.

Partitions create a quieter, more subdued dining area. Ornate lighting fixtures and delicately patterned glass and mirrors add sparkle to the room.

The bar is one of three distinct dining areas. The space possesses a feeling of warmth gained from the rich wood canopy and counter.

◊ The greenhouse/cafe area is a casual meeting place in which light meals are served.

CHAPTER 4

Delis, Fast Food and Quick Service Restaurants

Fast-food facilities meet the pace of today's schedules, their popularity being determined by the type of food and service offered. Maximum seating and fast turnover is especially encouraged by the chain restaurants, who maximize floor space and devise designs that do not invite lingering among customers. Durability and easy, inexpensive maintenance are major considerations. Tables, chairs, and floorings must withstand the heavy volume of customer traffic and must be easy for staff to handle.

The fast-food or deli restaurant need not be impersonal, however. The trend today is to create a pleasant dining experience and de-emphasize the assembly-line atmosphere. Touches of art, decorative wall fixtures, and theme designs can help warm the atmosphere. These designs, however, must be well planned and must work in combination with service operations, never apart from them.

McDonald's—Larchmont establishes a new prototype to celebrate the 30th anniversary of the chain. A black-and-white checkerboard motif is used to offset the park-like setting established by plantings, street-light poles, and wooden bench seating. Fine detailing is also used, an element of design rarely seen in fast-food places. The skylights, for example, are tiled with a checkerboard pattern, the edges mirrored and defined with rows of sparkling light bulbs. Seat upholstery, counter seating for singles, resin-covered fabric tabletops, and a complex lighting scheme distinguish this McDonald's from other fast-food facilities.

In the McDonald's—Vineland, a Victorian motif is amplified with patterned, custom-designed tile flooring; moveable chairs; softer lighting, intimate enclaves; and an increased number of tables for two. All of these things work to downplay the food-factory image and encourage the feeling of a pleasant dining experience.

A series of levels has been created to offer a variety of dining experiences at the New York Delicatessen. The stylized, richly colored Deco murals complement the refined, multicolor palette used in the furnishings and architectural elements. Carpeting has been installed for sound control. Light levels are balanced and softened, directly contrasting the harsh levels usually associated with a deli.

Small delis and food counters must incorporate eye-catching elements and allow merchandise to be visible instantly to attract customer attention. This is accomplished in a variety of ways: glass display cases, open kitchens, logos, and signage.

At Mickies, a fanciful, exciting environment is created through the use of pastel colors, neon, and giant, eye-catching food sculptures. The counter has been relocated near the mall corridor for quick and easy viewing by passersby.

The merchandise at C'est Delicious is clearly displayed on cookie sheets in a glass-enclosed display case, and enhanced by high-intensity spotlights. Enticing signage and graphics make the small food shop particularly attractive.

At New York Fries, the exposed cooking area creates interest. A pink laminated counter trimmed with thick, rounded wood, and a smattering of good-natured signs, such as the one explaining "The Birth of the Fry," give the space lighthearted appeal.

At Pizzeria Uno, the green-and-gold color scheme established on the exterior is carried throughout the interior, which resembles a sidewalk cafe. Use of street-light poles, shining brass, and shiny-clean tile floors give the interior a fresh, lively feeling. Warburton's Old World charm is projected through the rough-textured brick wall, photos and memorabilia, and delicately molded tables.

PIZZERIA UNO

Project Location: Allston, Massachusetts
Client: Uno Restaurants, Inc.
Interior Designers: Morris Nathanson, Peter Niemitz, (*project designers*), Morris Nathanson Design, Inc.
Photographer: Peter Vanderwalter

Pizzeria Uno took over a sandwich shop in a transitional residential area to establish the prototype restaurant for what would become the Pizzeria Uno chain. All of the elements in the design were considered carefully for adaptability to new and diverse locations. Imagery had to be strong and substantial.

To overcome any preconceived ideas, the interior is designed to look like a pub and to act as a social eating, drinking, and gathering place for young, professional clientele. The fresh, appealing green-and-gold color scheme begun on the exterior is carried through the interior. Globe-shaped wall-mounted lighting fixtures the street poles on the inside create the ambiance of a sidewalk cafe. The quality and sophistication of the environment is apparent in materials such as rich woods and brass.

The comfortable, street-like environment is created through globe-shaped wall-mounted lighting fixtures and street poles.

The bar area is on a raised platform separated from the main dining area by shining brass railing.

NEW YORK FRIES

Project Location: New York, New York
Client: Leonard Desser
Architect and Lighting Designer: Martin E. Dorf, Dorf Associates
Graphic Artist: Al Diorio, Al Diorio Design
Photographer: Alan Schindler, Alan Schindler Photography

New York Fries is a 400-square foot French fry operation located in Manhattan's South Street Seaport. The designer had to create an identifiable image that would stand out from the other similar, exposed concessions, mazimize sales, and serve as a prototype for potential expansion.

A bold, lighthearted monument to the potato has been developed and implemented. Marble, 6-inch curved bullnose wood trim, and classical shaping are contrasted with whimsical coloring to attract customers. Realistic, hand-carved wooden potatoes sit at the tops of the columns. Custom hoods and vertical stacking of mechanical equipment conserve space. The low-voltage lighting conserves energy and prolongs lamp life. The concession has been completed within a budget of approximately $130,000, including equipment.

The pink laminated counter is accented with thick bands of rounded wood trim and a double brass railing.

MCDONALD'S

Project Location: Vineland, New Jersey
Client: Harvey Dubin
Interior and Lighting Designer: Brad Elias, Hochheiser-Elias Design Group, Inc.
Photographer: Alan Schindler

Several features incorporated into the McDonald's, Vineland, signify a new direction in fast-food restaurant design. The flexible seating, moveable chairs, increased number of tables for two, and counter seating for singles create a more stylish dining environment, and downplay the fast-food factory image.

Postmodern architectural forms are used to create intimate enclaves and to update the Victorian motif required by the owner. Contemporary colors, such as mauve and teal, and natural materials add to the projection of a full-service type of restaurant atmosphere.

All materials and details, though fashionable, still meet strict McDonald's corporate standards for cleaning and durability. The quality custom-designed floor tile, for example, is attractive and practical.

The lighting system includes indirect and incandescent accents. While encouraging brisk turnover, it is softer than the typical lighting of fast-food restaurants.

With scarce product differentiation among fast-food chains, design of the dining facilities has become the marketing tool of the 1980s, and McDonald's is on the leading edge.

The Victorian motif required by the owner is carried through in details such as the patterned, custom-designed tile flooring.

Intimate enclaves and more tables for two promote the feeling of a dining experience, and downplay the stereotypical assembly-line image.

McDONALD'S

Project Location: Larchmont, New Jersey
Client: Don Smith
Interior and Lighting Designer: Brad Elias, Hochheiser-Elias Design Group, Inc.
Photographer: Peter Paige, Peter Paige Associates

McDonald's—Larchmont is one of 30 McDonald's restaurants nationwide chosen to serve as a new architectural prototype in commemoration of the company's 30th anniversary. While it was necessary to work within McDonald's rigid requirements for maintenance and durability, the client requested that an innovative approach be given to the standard fast-food design. A neutral backdrop was also requested, so that a fresh look could be created by simply changing the artwork, upholstery, and wallcovering. Architectural problems included the greenhouse built on the south side of the building, which caused an uncomfortably high sun load, and the skylights, which were deeply recessed into the 10-foot-high ceiling and broken up by structural beams.

A park-like setting is created through the use of wooden seating, plantings, and decorative pole light fixtures.

A complex lighting system has been installed which includes decorative street lamps, rows of exposed bulbs, fluorescent and incandescent wall fixtures, back-lit stained glass panels, and recessed low-voltage units fitted with colored gels.

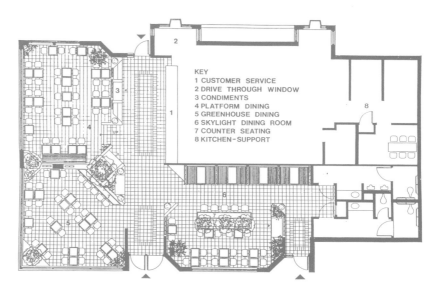

KEY
1 CUSTOMER SERVICE
2 DRIVE THROUGH WINDOW
3 CONDIMENTS
4 PLATFORM DINING
5 GREENHOUSE DINING
6 SKYLIGHT DINING ROOM
7 COUNTER SEATING
8 KITCHEN-SUPPORT

Rows of sparkling bulbs, checkerboard tiling, mirrored edges, and trough planters below them make the skylights significant architectural elements in the space.

C'EST DELICIOUS

Project Location: New York, New York
Client: Angelo Katapolis
Architect: Martin E. Dorf, Dorf Associates
Lighting Designer: Steve Bernstein, Cline, Bettridge, Bernstein
Graphic Artist: Carol Drazen
Photographer: Alan Schindler, Alan Schindler Photography

An attractive, eye-catching snack shop had to be created in a 200 square-foot space at Herald Center in New York City to house the baked goods, coffee, sandwiches, and desserts for sale.

Baked goods are both stored and displayed on cookie sheets in glass cases below the glass counters. Visible storage enhances the impression that the goods are freshly made, and allows maximum visibility of foods available to passersby. The enticing, colorful signage and graphics also attract potential customers. A mirrored wall behind the counters makes the space seem larger than it is. High-intensity spotlights aid in attracting attention to the products. The shop was completed with a budget of approximately $90,000.

The 200 square foot specialty shop contains custom-designed glass display cases. Merchandise is spotlighted by high-intensity lighting units.

MUFFINS
CAKES
SCONES
PIES
CROISSANTS
PASTRIES

MICKIE'S

Project Location: Plattsburgh, New York
Client: Mark Dame (*president*)
Architect and Lighting Designer: Martin E. Dorf, Dorf Associates
Graphic Artist: Carol Drazen
Photographer: Alan Schindler, Alan Schindler Photography

The existing Mickie's restaurant had been experiencing poor sales. The layout prevented customers' visual contact with food, and the atmosphere of the space was dull and lifeless. The objective of renovating the 2,000 square foot restaurant was to increase sales through the creation of an exciting, fanciful environment that would serve also as a prototype for possible expansion.

The food counter has been relocated parallel to the mall corridor to increase visual contact with food items. Pastel colors, neon, accent lighting, and oversized food sculptures are combined to form a new, upbeat, friendly image for the family restaurant.

Glass sneeze-guard panels provide protection and maximum visibility for food. Low voltage lighting reduces electrical bills and prolongs lamp life. The renovation has been accomplished within a budget of approximately $75,000, which includes general construction, finishes, furniture, lighting and kitchen equipment.

This 2000 square foot space is a renovation of an existing restaurant.

THE NEW YORK DELICATESSEN

Project Location: New York, New York

Client: Ralph Rosenblum

Interior and Lighting Designer: Brad Elias, Hochheiser-Elias Design Group, Inc.

Photographer: Peter Paige, Peter Paige Associates

The New York Delicatessen is housed in a two-story space with 5,500 square feet on the ground level and 3,000 square feet on the balcony level. The owner required that the large space not look empty when occupied by only a few people, and that finish materials possess the same maintenance-free qualities found in any lesser-quality delicatessen.

The delicatessen is broken up into distinct areas to provide a more humanistic quality to the space, and to avoid an empty feeling during slow hours. The space is divided into a series of levels to provide varied dining experiences. The levels increase in height reaching upward until, standing on the long platform, identified by the double stairway, one can touch the balcony level.

Special care has been taken to balance light levels to provide a well-illuminated space that does not offer the harsh lighting usually associated with a deli.

The restaurant is broken up into several multi-level spaces to accommodate varied dining experiences. The waiters' stations are located beneath the central elevated statue display.

To add warmth to the space, every metallic surface is finished in brass or gold metallic. The attention to detail is evident in the variety of textures and colors blended in this small niche.

A warm color scheme has been chosen—varied shades of cream and burgundy, with teal, rose, and French vanilla accents.

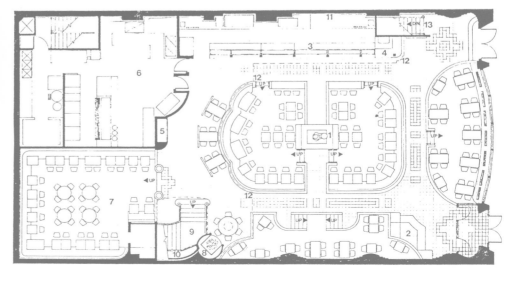

Tucked under the balcony, separate
from the other dining areas, is a
"quiet room" which seats 65 and uses
a softer range of materials.

WARBURTON'S

Project Location: Boston, Massachusetts
Client: Warburton's, Inc.
Interior Designers: Peter Niemitz, Blase Gallo, Morris
Nathanson, (*project designer*), Morris
Nathanson Design, Inc.
Photographer: Warren Jagger

The design of the Warburton's store derives much of its inspiration from a Bond Street, London, specialty shop, with added touches of what Americans perceive as English style.

Several messages were to be conveyed through the shop's interior and exterior: quality baked goods are sold here, the product is fresh, and baking is done on the premises. To achieve this, careful attention is given to details which combine Old World charm with a casual, food-is-served-fast atmosphere. They include elements such the golden muffin finials, belt sign, graphics, packaging, and the artwork telling Warburton's history.

The store is planned so that its four major areas—food preparation, food display, sales service, and the cafe—function well together. Because the space requirements for these areas were anticipated to vary with each subsequent location of a Warburton's shop, the Warburton's Bakery and Cafe prototype was conceived with enough design flexibility to allow easy adaptation.

*Details such as the gold muffin finials,
the belt sign, and the blue and white
tile floor, reflect the casual, fast-food
nature of the establishment.*

Old World charm is reflected through old prints and photos, painted bricks and ornate cafe-style tables.

CHAPTER 5

Bars, Lounges and Clubs

Clubs do offer food service to their patrons but, more often than not, the main attraction is the fun that goes hand-in-hand with brisk beverage sales. Eating facilities in clubs function primarily as "holding rooms" for the dancing or socializing that usually follows. Ideally, a club's restaurant should be situated at a vantage point from which diners can view the dance area. At the same time, it must be near the entrance, where people entering the premises may be seen. People-watching is the foremost activity that a club design should enhance, both by promoting crowd circulation and by keeping visibility paths clear.

To increase revenues during off-peak hours, some clubs make available areas for parties, catered luncheons, and fashion shows. Their sophisticated lighting and sound systems are a part of this flexible use of space, accommodating a variety of functions. In this, lighting is a critical design element, as it must function well for both daytime and evening activities. It must be subtle enough to provide a sophisticated atmosphere for daytime lunches, and exciting enough to accentuate the social whirl of a dance-filled night.

At Touch, architectural elements establish the design rhythms. The dance lounge is dramatically heightened by a skylight above a marble floor. Exterior plantings and interior palm trees visually combine to create the romantic effect of garden dancing under a moonlit sky.

At Caffe Luna, the casual, elegant feeling of a Northern Italian sidewalk cafe is created in the use of earthy colors, stucco textures, frescoes, and black and white tiling. The imagery depicted in the decor—sky, night, moon, and stars—reflects the celestial name of the club.

The fun, tropical environment at Key West is established through the skillful blend of mixed architectural elements—rococo door frames, exposed ductwork, hand-painted tables, neon, and oversized carpet patterns in a variety of colors.

The color palette of the Utah Jazz "100" Club is neutral and minimal to allow patrons to be the center of attention. The linear layout of the club allows for future growth and for expansion of activities. Service areas, a dining room, a bar/lounge, a boardroom, and intimate gathering places are all included in the club.

The several distinct areas that comprise Pete & Martys collectively create for patrons the impression that they are walking down a city street, free to sample a variety of foods and entertainment. The nostalgic and street-like environment is engulfed in a melange of props, including hubcaps on chainlink fences, 1960s guitars, and 1950s portable radios.

The punk interior of Bandito Ditto has almost no decor. The black, white, and red color scheme is warmed by wooden flooring and settees. A jagged red streak is the focal point, and is repeated on the floor, the bar, and in the neon logo. A fragmented architectural approach complements the intended use of the space—distinct areas for varying functions.

Caroline's, too, is divided into three distinct areas—a club, a dining area, and a bar—and is designed using industrial-style materials for a clean, modern look.

The trompe l'oeil of Sgarlato's Cafe depicts a street scene reminiscent of those found on the Italian Riviera. Marble and ceramic tile floor, marble tabletops, plantings and cafe-style chairs create an outdoor cafe feeling.

TOUCH

Project Location: Los Angeles, California
Owner: Hugh Hefner
Interior Designer: Stanley Felderman, Leason Pomeroy Felderman Associates

Dining Room Booths, Armchairs, Banquettes, Mural, and Sandblasted Design: Stanley Felderman Custom Design
Kitchen Consultant: Ennis & McJunkin
General Contractor: Illig Construction Company

When Hugh Hefner, the Playboy empire founder, created the Touch Club, he wanted a place with the look and flavor of the elegant clubs of the 1930s. He asked designer Stanley Felderman to execute his plans for the club in an existing structure, and to establish a sense of balance and symmetry evoking a soothing, comforting quality. An architectural ordering and shaping of the environment was subsequently realized in two recurring themes: visual awareness of space beyond, and a progression of structural rhythms.

Entering the club, the patron is made to feel exclusive by the filter-like compression at the entrance, and the dramatic volumetric expansions that follow reaffirm the notion that to enter is to be special.

All of this luxury creates a mood to touch (as in "touch dancing"), and guests are encouraged to be a participant in the overall club experience.

Structural elements, such as the truncated columns between the passageway and the dining room, contribute a sense of increased scale and grandeur to the environment.

Ceiling coves outlined in blue visually break up the large area. Formal barriers between spaces do not exist.

Details, such as the etched glass, ceiling fixtures, and wall mouldings, are ornate and form an interesting contrast to the basic, modern architectural lines.

CAFE BA-BA-REEBA

Project Location:	Chicago, Illinois
Client:	Lettuce Entertain You Enterprises (Richard Melman, Marv Magid, Gabino Sotelino)
Interior Designers:	Bill J. Aumiller, Jeff Everett, Maureen McFarlane, Mary Timm, Charles Bennett, Richard Melman, Aumiller Youngquist, P.C.
Architect:	Bill J. Aumiller, Aumiller Youngquist, P.C.
Contractor:	Capitol Construction
Mechanical Engineer:	G & C Consulting Engineers
Photographer:	Mark Ballogg, Steinkamp & Ballogg Photography

Cafe Ba-Ba-Reeba is the first tapas bar in Chicago, and is patterned after the pre-dinner, eating/drinking places known for lively conversation and common to Spain. The design concept provides a variety of settings where patrons are able to view and select the tapas-style appetizers along with their drinks. Dining and drinking areas are inter-mixed in a series of rooms, each spilling into the next to encourage circulation.

Open kitchen areas and food/liquor displays help maintain the informal, easy-going atmosphere.

Dining areas are located to take full advantage of the outdoor dining/garden areas when the weather permits.

The restaurant is housed in three buildings joined together. For this reason, major structural modifications were necessary to connect the dining areas. Fire shutters had to be installed to comply with safety regulations.

The connection of the three major dining areas promotes the display of food in different settings and invites patrons to explore the varied environments.

Shown is the Tapas bar #1 viewed from the entry. Color and interest are added by the food displays and patterned tile and marble.

Behind the counter is a wood-burning oven. Drinking and dining sections, open kitchen areas, and food/liquor displays are interwoven throughout the restaurant.

The bar in one of the dining rooms is enhanced by a skylight. Decorative details include a Picasso-inspired mural, and wrought-iron door grilles. The open back bar can be separated from the dining area behind it by sliding glass panels.

The restaurant is patterned after establishments in Spain that promote a happy mixture of eating, drinking, and conversation.

Shown is one of several food displays, and "The First Tapas" mural. Pitchers of sangria are kept in refrigerated cases at the bar.

CAFFE LUNA

Project Location: Newton, Massachusetts
Client: Luna Restaurants, Ltd.
Interior Designers: Blase Gallo, Peter Niemitz, Morris Nathanson, (*project designers*), Morris Nathanson Design, Inc.
Photographer: Warren Jagger

At Caffe Luna, the romance of a Northern Italian sidewalk cafe is recalled in earthy colors, stucco textures, and frescoes of the type seen in Florence, and in the black and white tiles imitating those seen in the Duomo of Sienna. Other imagery in the restaurant is derived from its name, which conjures visions of a night sky filled with moon and stars. The designers chose planetary spheres and a faux-painted starlit sky to create the aura of an evening at an Italian outdoor cafe. Pedestals with inner-lit columns establish an architectural rhythm and affect the ruins of Rome—a perfect and natural design complement to the theme of astrology, the science born in Italy.

The plan of Caffe Luna had to follow the programmed objectives of the owner's specific requirements. The beer, wine, and champagne bar is up front, visible, and typically European; it acts as a congenial meeting place and as a reception and holding area. The take-out counter is immediately accessible from the entrance, and does not interfere with internal restaurant service. While the rotisserie is completely visible to patrons, the kitchen is visible only above a certain level, where patrons can see activity, but not actual food preparation.

The budget for the entire project, including two storefronts and excluding kitchen equipment, was $250,000.

A focal point is the faux-painted sky, [and the pedestals integrated with light.

The European-style beer, wine and champagne bar is up front, very visible, and an appropriate meeting place and holding area.

The take-out counter is accessible to the front and does not interfere with restaurant service. Earthy colors, stucco textures, and black and white tiles, reminiscent of the Duomo of Siena, are used throughout.

KEY WEST

Project Location: Boston, Massachusetts
Client: Barnsider Management Corporation
Interior Designers: Blase Gallo, Peter Niemitz, Morris Nathanson, (*project designers*), Morris Nathanson Design, Inc.
Photographer: Warren Jagger

The owners of Key West felt that this new restaurant in the chain had to be unique to be successful in its environment—a very competitive college market. The only location available was an unusual space on the second floor of Kenmore Square, adjacent to Boston University. Structural limitations included a maze of columns with no pattern, a curved front to the building, and walls of which no two were parallel.

The designers created a decidedly fun, tropical environment filled with colorful, artistic elements; these include original silk-screen prints emblazoned with bright tropical colors and exotic themes. The mixed architectural elements—some existed in the space, others were added—include rococo door frames, exposed ductwork, and post-modern shapes. Hand-painted tables, bands of neon, vinyl asbestos tile, and oversized carpet patterns complete the bold design.

The bar adjoins the main entrance and is the predominant feature of the space. The multi-colored neon has been custom designed.

The colorful tabletops are hand painted. The restaurant serves lunch and dinner, and is transformed into a disco at night.

The tropical atmosphere is established at the entrance via the soft colors, ceiling fans, and pink flamingos.

The ceiling is suspended acoustical tile. Due to column placement, two raised platforms have been positioned at oblique angles to each other and the bar.

A mixture of architectural elements is used, such as the rococo door frames, exposed ductwork, post-modern shapes, and oversized carpet patterns.

BANDITO
DITTO

Project Location: New York, New York
Client: Rudy Mosney
Interior and Lighting Designer: Brad Elias, Hochheiser-Elias Design Group, Inc.
Photographer: Nancy Scariati

Bandito Ditto, housed in a space that was formerly a storefront occupied by a Chinese restaurant, is a New Wave Mexican restaurant that avoids typical Mexican decor—hanging plants, cactus, blankets—in favor of an austere, "punk" environment with a striking black, white, and red color scheme, and virtually no decor.

The 50-foot-long, 24-foot-deep space includes greenhouse dining, entertainment, and intimate dining areas, and a large bar for socializing. The restaurant is also designed to accommodate art shows, a requirement prompted by the owner's interest in art.

The ceiling height varies and is very low in some areas. The bar, for example, is on a platform with a 7-foot-high ceiling.

To make the ceiling appear higher, faux cement coffers have been installed between the beams. Sheet-rock wings with built-in cove lighting are layered below the coffers to create the illusion of greater coffer height.

Distinct, separate environments are created throughout space. In the greenhouse, for example, a fragmented architectural approach is repeated in glass and stucco. Unifying elements include a red streak found on the floor and on the bar, built into the outsized columns, and incorporated into the neon logo. The streak reflects the restaurant's name and "punk" theme—a bandito like Zorro, and the streak of red in someone's hair.

One of the unifying themes is a jagged red streak, which appears on the floor, bar, columns, and in the neon logo.

The design is based on the interplay of black and red. Most of the lighting consists of adjustable, recessed low-voltage fixtures.

The owner did not want decorative
elements used that would reflect a
typical Mexican restaurant—hanging
plants, cacti, or Mexican blankets.
Consequently, decor is virtually
nonexistent. The distinctive streak of
red appears in the column.

Between the ceiling beams, faux
cement coffers have been installed.
Below the coffers, sheet-rock wings
with built-in cove lighting have been
added, making the ceiling appear
higher than it is.

CAROLINE'S

Project Location: New York, New York
Client: Caroline Hirsch, (*president*)
Architect: Martin E. Dorf, Dorf Associates
Lighting Designer: Domingo Gonzalez Design
Graphic Artist: Alfred de la Houssaye, Alfred de la Houssaye Design
Photographer: Mark Ross, Mark Ross Photography

Caroline's, a 10,000-square-foot trilevel comedy club/restaurant/bar/cafe is located at South Street Seaport's Pier 17 in Manhattan. The first level contains a 150-seat cafe, with outdoor seating on the Pier, and a 50-foot terrazzo bar. The bar, which is rear-illuminated, features a raw-bar display area and an exposed grilling station.

Caroline's was conceived as an open, theatrical space that would combine the excitement of a comedy club with an equally electric bar and restaurant. Customers would be encouraged to experience an entire night's entertainment under one roof.

The comedy club section is designed to be a state-of-the-art television studio for remote broadcasting of comedy acts and other entertainment specials. Professional lighting and sound equipment are included to make this space easily convertible to a production facility. Lunch, light dinners, and drinks are served in this room. In addition, the room is used for corporate functions year round.

This open, theatrical environment is further enhanced by a breathtaking view of lower Manhattan, the East River, and Brooklyn Heights, making Caroline's one of the most exciting nightspots in New York City.

The glass-enclosed coat room in the 25-foot atrium is separated from the club by a floor to ceiling clear glass wall.

The club is designed to provide patrons with an entire evening's dining and entertainment. Lunch and light dinners are served in the club area, which is used also for corporate functions.

The first level seats 150 and contains
a 50-foot terrazzo bar. There is
outdoor seating on the pier as well.

The spiral staircase leads to the dressing room and general manager's office on the third level.

Comedy greats, such as Lucille Ball, Desi Arnaz, and Stan Laurel, are depicted in the colorful murals.

The club room is a state of the art studio which is equipped with special lighting and sound equipment to accommodate remote broadcasts of comedy acts and other entertainment.

UTAH JAZZ "100" CLUB

Project Location:	Salt Lake City, Utah
Client:	Utah Jazz
Interior and Lighting Designer:	Gensler and Associates/Architects
Architect:	Bonneville Architects
General Contractor:	Daw Incorporated
Mechanical Engineer:	CCI Mechanical
Millwork:	Custom Design
Photographer:	Gordon Peery

The conversion of a storage area of the Salt Palace Convention Center in Salt Lake City to a social and dining space was the challenge faced in designing the Utah Jazz "100" Club. This space serves as a clubhouse for active contributors to the Utah Jazz Basketball season. The place needed not only maximum flexibility to accommodate various large banquets and functions, but also the ability to expand 100 percent with minimum remodeling.

The inherent geometry of the convention center strengthens the function of the semi-circular pathway that connects the open dining area, the board room which also serves as a function room for private parties, and the bar/lounge area. When expansion plans materialize, the bar area will be centrally located.

Lighting is an important element in establishig the mood. Indirect, direct and wall-washing fixtures were combined to allow for flexibility of atmosphere. To reinforce the Club's purpose of rewarding contributors, the color palette has been kept neutral and minimal so that the people and the activity in the room become the focal points.

Uncluttered passageways unite the dining areas, board room, lounge/bar, service areas, and intimate gathering places. The spaces have been designed to incorporate 100-percent expansion with a minimum amount of renovation.

The large, open spaces are flexible and make it easy to accommodate a variety of functions.

The space planning is based on the structure and geometry of the Salt Palace.

PETE AND MARTY'S

Project Location: Anjou, Quebec, Canada
Interior Designers: Robert J. DiLeonardo, Thomas R. Limone, DiLeonardo International
Photographer: Warren Jagger, Warren Jagger Photography

Pete and Marty's is the Quebecois version of a highly successful, multi-level dining/dancing restaurant. The brick and steel factory-type structure is located in the Les Halles d'Anjou, the chic new farmers market/office complex in a suburb of Montreal. The street-environment design encourages customers to "graze" and to float from one area to another; it is a refinement of the original "Pete and Marty's" in Toronto.

The restaurant/club is designed to make customers feel that they are walking down a city street, free to experience choices in food and entertainment. Customers can stroll from the Diner, to Le Hot Club, to the outdoor dining and dancing area in warm weather, to the Back Street Bar. Patrons can eat a full meal or a snack, call a date at a phone booth, enjoy 1950s music at Le Hot Club, or select soul music from a jukebox.

The designers created a neo-realistic environment by using "honest materials" such as hubcaps, chain-link fences, tin ceilings, and period colors like "Coca Cola red" and electric blue. Nostalgic props—1960s guitars, 1950s radios, an old-fashioned television painted on a wall—are scattered through the club. Neon signage and spray-painted graffiti add touches of fantasy that have helped to make the club a success with the young and spirited clientele.

In The Back Street section, a street environment is created with eye-catching items such as the hubcap-covered wall.

Nostalgia-inspiring details include counters tiled on the top and side and an old-time Coca Cola vending machine.

Guitars from the 1960s and a jukebox
are found in The Diner.

Old-fashioned radios, and 1950s television sets painted on the wall adorn Le Hot Club.

Customers are encouraged to float
from one section of the club to another
and to experience the varied types of
atmosphere and entertainment
available.

SGARLATOS CAFE

Project Location: New York, New York
Client: Rocco Sgarlato
Interior and Lighting Designer: Brad Elias, Hochheiser-Elias Design Group, Inc.
Photographer: Nancy Scariati

Sgarlato's Cafe aimed to attract both the considerable business clientele of the area, known to favor light lunches and cocktails, and the South Street Seaport's many informally dressed tourists and shoppers, who make serendipitous stops for lunch and dinner. Though Sgarlato's is less expensive than its adjacent rivals, the cafe nevertheless needed to exhibit high style to draw patrons away from the competition, and to fulfill the requirements of the mall.

Since no lighting could be attached to the greenhouse ceiling, the restaurant is illuminated with indirect quartz uplights mounted on structural columns, and with an indirect neon cove that runs along the one solid wall.

Part of the dining space consists of an "outdoor" cafe-style area that extends into the mall. The client's extensive requirements for the kitchen, storage areas, restrooms, seating, and service stations made it necessary for the bar to project out beyond the store line and into the mall as well. However, because both the bar and cafe must be secured at night with the mall's standard rolling gate, a split in the *trompe l'oeil* marble of the bar was made to provide a track through which the gate passes to safeguard both the liquor and the cafe entrance.

Since no lighting could be attached to the greenhouse ceiling, indirect quartz uplights and an indirect neon cove along the one solid wall have been installed.

The lighting and interior design have been planned carefully so as not to interrupt the spectacular view of the Brooklyn Bridge. Fifty percent of the cafe's walls and ceiling are glass.

The trompe l'oeil *street scene mimics buildings along the Italian Riviera where plain stucco buildings are adorned with architectural details painted on in* trompe l'oeil *style.*

CHAPTER
6

Restorations

The high costs of new construction and real estate and the tax breaks available to those who restore buildings have made restoration projects an inviting alternative for many restaurants. Most of these historical sites also offer an intrinsic atmosphere and character that no amount of decorating and styling can equal.

Restorations require quality workmanship and reproductions. All of these undertakings call for meticulous supervision in order to comply with stringent safety codes. Many are subjected to strict guidelines and intense review and planning boards. Restorations, consequently, can involve considerable time and enormous expense.

OLD LYME
INN RESTAURANT

Project Location: Old Lyme, Connecticut
Client/Designer: Diana Field Atwood
Photographers: Roland Laine, Saybrook Studio;
Daniel Lucente

The inn's new owner decided to restore the building to its original elegance and to furnish it with antiques of the period and works of turn-of-the-century artists. The entire interior of the building was gutted and then rebuilt from the ground up, as the structure itself was unstable. Over the years, most of the interior walls and staircases had been relocated or removed. The Inn, purchased in 1976, had previously operated as a marginal Italian restaurant. Only the exterior of the building reflected its historic district location and Empire period construction. The interior, due to fire and negligence, was barely recognizable as a once-elegant Old Lyme home.

The main dining room is adorned with rich blue carpeting and chairs, gold damask wallpaper, and reproduction Victorian chandeliers.

THE
MANSION

Project Location:	Atlanta, Georgia
Client:	Bill Swearingen, (*president*), The Mansion Restaurant
Interior and Lighting Designer:	Bill Swearingen, (*president*), The Mansion Restaurant
Architect:	Alan Salzman, Alan Salzman & Associates
Photographer:	Larry Thomas, Larry Thomas Photography

Though The Mansion was established as a restaurant in 1970, the building was constructed over a century ago, in 1885. It occupies a full city block, close to downtown Atlanta, Georgia. The structure is a prime example of the High Victorian Shingle Style of architecture.

Each of the dining areas is decorated and furnished in its own unique way. For example, The Library is paneled with tooled leather, and adorned with gesso embossing. In addition to the eleven indoor dining rooms, patrons can enjoy outdoor dining in The Courtyard, with its water-lilly filled pond and refreshing fountain. Nightly entertainment is offered in The Gazebo.

It is the attention to detail that promotes in the diner the feeling of being in a grand and classic Southern home: ornately carved banisters, lush plants, period furniture, elegantly appointed fireplaces, wall-hung portraits, and floral-patterned draperies and carpeting.

Due to the number and variety of spaces in The Mansion, a large range of functions, including business lunches, dinners, weddings, cocktail parties, receptions, fashion shows, and other special occasions, can be accommodated. The American cuisine includes Southern specialties.

The Mansion restaurant was established in 1970 and is located on a full city block, close to downtown Atlanta.

The original structure of The Mansion was built in 1885 with high Victorian-style shingle architecture. The ornate, arched, white frame and beautiful lighting fixtures enhance this dining area—one of 11 dining rooms in The Mansion.

Attention to detail brings out the Victorian character—well-kept plantings, cozy chair and table, wall-mounted portraits, and ornate banister.

Patrons can enjoy outdoor dining near a refreshing pond and entertainment from the gazebo in the large, open courtyard.

The home-like environment makes patrons' visits comfortable and relaxing. Note the detailed fireplace, flower-patterned carpeting, and rich, velvet-upholstered chairs.

Delicate archways and a pastel-colored ceiling reflect the classic Southern atmosphere of this light and airy room.

CHAPTER

7

The New American Diner

The diner, an American tradition, is making a comeback in the 1980s. The motivation for this trend is twofold:

- nostalgia for the relatively carefree years of the 1930s, -40s, and -50s, when the popularity of the diner was at its peak, and
- a consumer craving for the fast, efficient, individual, yet moderately priced service that diners of the past had a reputation of offering.

Several diners featured in this chapter specifically aim to recreate the atmosphere of the 1950s.

Ed Debevic's Short Orders Deluxe is a replica interpretation of the classic '50s look. The long, narrow diner car is furnished with red vinyl booths and chrome coat racks. The open kitchen, fully appointed soda fountain, and melange of '50s signage and memorabilia establish the lighthearted, nostalgic atmosphere.

Bette's Oceanview also has been designed with an informal '50s look. Rather than relying heavily on memorabilia, however, this diner concentrates on the use of authentic '50s diner materials such as linen formica, chrome strips, and aluminum moldings. The pink, black, and red color scheme and the black-and-white diamond-patterned flooring are throwbacks to the heyday of the original diners. The predominance of hard surfaces—linoleum, plaster, formica, and stainless steel—increases the noise and, consequently, the energy level.

Edie's Diner also uses black-and-white checkerboard flooring, red vinyl booths, and chrome coat racks. Stainless-steel panels with a starburst design, old photos, and lighting fixtures reinforce the '50s flavor.

Today's diner may incorporate the atmosphere of a past era, but it does not ignore the design and menu choices that appeal to the clientele of the '80s. The Hollywood Diner, though based on the White Town diner chain popular in the 1920s and -30s, is designed to project a neighborhood eatery image and to appeal to a more upscale, refined clientele. The neighborhood eatery style is embodied in items such as the jukebox, milk-shake mixers,

television, bowls of popcorn, jars of candy, and related memorabilia. The upscale clientele is attracted by the fresh flowers on each table, flattering pink-tone lighting from chrome wall sconces, and soft carpeting designed to lower the noise level. The menu wisely reflects the appetite of today's patron as well. A mixture is offered: traditional fare, such as hamburgers and hot dogs, and more gourmet-style specialites, such as oysters on the half-shell and swordfish sandwiches.

Present-day diners combine yesterday's fun with modern familiarity. Patrons are secure in the knowledge that they can order basic American fare at good prices and at the same time be entertained by and enjoy the ambiance. While there is danger of over-saturation in the market, it is safe to assume that diners will always mean something special to the American public and therefore enjoy patronage for a long time.

EDIE'S DINER

Project Location: Marina del Rey, California
Interior Designers: Charlie Sparks (*principal-in-charge*), Bob Felten (*project manager*), Schafer Associates, Inc.; and Stevie Bannister, (*principal-in-charge*), Bruce Martenay (*project manager*), Andrea Diaz (*color and materials*), Schafer Associates West, Inc.
General Contractor: Jack Willingham, Willingham/Wilson
Photographers: Mark Milroy and Mary McAleer, Milroy/McAleer

The pre-existing space of Edie's Diner was that of an "ocean theme" coffee shop attached to its sister restaurant, Casola's Fish House. To provide the establishment with its own identity, the designers created a vibrant, attractive 1950s-style diner.

The exterior is treated with stainless-steel and gloss-white painted metal panels. Stainless-steel panels with a starburst design and gloss block wall adorn the entry. The facade is illuminated at night from fixtures installed beneath a translucent, cerulean-blue awning.

In the interior, the 1950s theme is carried through, mainly in the black and white checkerboard flooring. Red vinyl booths, black-granite plastic laminate table tops, and chrome coat racks at each booth authenticate the "diner" look.

The counter is made of black-granite plastic laminate with polished aluminum trim. The footrest is of black and white ceramic tile. Chrome stools with red upholstery complete the counter. The walls are clad with stainless-steel panels with starburst designs, or are painted a semi-gloss white and adorned with photographs relating to the 1950s. Pendant-hung light fixtures have chrome stems and discs in 1950s globe style.

The pendant-hung light fixtures used have chrome stems and 1950s-style globes. Photographs relating to the 1950s adorn the walls.

A 1950s look is created through the combination of black-and-white checkerboard flooring, red vinyl channelback booths, black granite plastic laminate table tops, and chrome coat racks at each booth.

Some of the walls are covered with stainless-steel panels decorated with starburst designs. Others are painted a semi-gloss white.

HOLLYWOOD DINER

Project Location: Los Angeles, California
Client: Patrick A. Terrail
Interior and Lighting Designer, and Architect: Patrick A. Terrail, My Management
Photographer: Francois Duhamel, SYGMA

The Hollywood Diner, located on Fairfax Avenue in Los Angeles, is contained in an aqua and white building that once housed the California Bridge Club. Although the Deco-style design of the interior is based on diners in the White Town chain built throughout the eastern U.S. during the 1920s and 1930s, a more refined, romantic, upscale, and idealized version is presented.

The two-counter diner is approximately 3,000 square feet and seats about 80. The front room, which has a combination wine bar, oyster bar, and soda fountain, is separated from the larger dining room by a glass panel.

The larger room has a longer eating counter with old-fashioned metal diner stools, and ceiling fans trimmed in glass. Shining copper pots hang from the ceiling in the open kitchen behind the counter.

The diner walls are white Formica trimmed with metal. The ceiling is pressed tin. Blue-grey vinyl banquettes line the walls and surround black Formica-topped tables. Comfortably cushioned chairs have arched, Deco-style metal backs.

The flavor of a casual neighborhood eatery is projected through details such as the jukebox, milk-shake mixers, television, bowls of popcorn, jars of candy, and related memorabilia.

An upscale image is maintained by details including fresh flowers on every table, soft carpeting for a quieter environment, and flattering pink-toned lighting that glows from half-sphere chrome wall sconces.

The diner is designed to be a more refined version of the White Town Chain of diners built in the 1920s and 1930s. The diner seats 80.

BETTE'S OCEANVIEW DINER

Project Location: Berkeley, California

Client: Bette Caminez

Interior Designers: Sue Conley, Bette Caminez, Manfred Kroning, Denny Abrams, Rick Milliken and Dave Kent, Abrams, Milliken & Kent

Architect: Abrams, Milliken & Kent

Lighting Designer: Carol Culver, Peerless Lighting

Photographer: Charles Frizzell

Bette's Oceanview Diner, the first revival diner on the West Coast, incorporates the best features of diners known in the 1930s, 1940s, and 1950s and satisfies the need for a moderately priced, neighborhood restaurant that is strikingly attractive yet unintimidating.

To create a diner with a familiar atmosphere, materials authentic to the period of the 1950s are used, such as linen formica, chrome stripping, and aluminum mouldings. The long and narrow shape of the 20-foot by 50-foot diner dictated that the black and white diamond-patterned vinyl floor tiles be hand cut to make them proportionate to the space. Red, pink, and black, colors strongly identified with the 1950s, are used as accents.

The design of the counter is the single most critical element in the plan: it gives the interior its proper form and establishes the linear quality of the dining space. The overhang above it functions as storage and creates a feeling of intimacy for customers seated at the counter. The metal-strip accenting and cove of plaster create a streamlined appearance reminiscent of a railway dining car.

The hard surfaces in Bette's amplify counter and table-top sounds, encouraging conversing customers to speak with heightened volume and helping to mask the noise of the kitchen. The high ceilings create an open feeling and enable maximum seating without patrons feeling cramped or claustrophobic.

The pink, red and black color scheme of the 20 by 50 foot space is reminiscent of the 1950s. The black and white diamond-patterned vinyl floor tiles have been hand cut to fit the space.

The 50s atmosphere is reflected in period materials used, such as the linen formica, chrome strips, and aluminum moldings.

The plaster, stainless steel, formica,
linoleum, and other hard surfaces
increase the noise level which produces
the dual effect of masking kitchen
sounds and intensifying the energy level
in the diner.

ED DEBEVIC'S SHORT ORDERS DELUXE

Project Location:	Deerfield, Illinois
Client:	Lettuce Entertain You Enterprises, and Collins Foods International, Inc.
Interior and Lighting Designer, and Architect:	Bill Aumiller, Aumiller Youngquist, P.C.
Design Consultant:	Alfred Baumann, RADIO
Contractor:	Capitol Construction
Engineering:	Diversified Engineering Services, Inc.
Photographer:	Mark Ballogg, Steincamp-Ballogg Photography

The problem of marketing two adjoining restaurants that serve distinctly different food types—Ed Debevic's Short Orders Deluxe and Shaw's Blue Crab—in one building was solved by imbuing each restaurant with its own distinct personality. (See Chapter 8, Seafood and Ocean Theme Restaurants, for Shaw's Blue Crab.)

Separate identities for each restaurant begin on the building's exterior. Color banding, in turquoise-green for Ed Debevic's and deep red for Shaw's Blue Crab, runs along the neutral-colored glazed concrete block of the exterior. These color identities are carried through, into the lobby. Additional differentiations seen from the exterior are Ed Debevic's diner car shape and Shaw's corner tower and pond.

Ed Debevic's embodies an interpretation of a classic 1950s diner. The soda fountain, diner car, and open kitchen are used to reinforce the nostalgic ideal. Materials like glazed concrete block, neon, plastic laminates in typical 1950s patterns, glass block—plus a light-hearted approach to color, light fixtures, and signage—create the brisk, clean atmosphere and convivial spirit of the 1950s.

The 50s theme is reinforced by a fully ◁ appointed soda fountain, neon signage, and metallic vertical surfaces on the counter front.

tain Service
Cocktails
ICE CREAM SODAS
MALTS
YOU EVER BEEN HAPPIER THAN YOU ARE RIGHT NOW?
NO BETTING
MORE ICE COLD
Mm-m-m
OUR MALT
Ladies Served First
The CUSTOMER IS Usually RIGHT

The main dining area is divided up by
low partitions.

The hostess desk sits amid a melange of polka-dot flooring, signage and memorabilia.

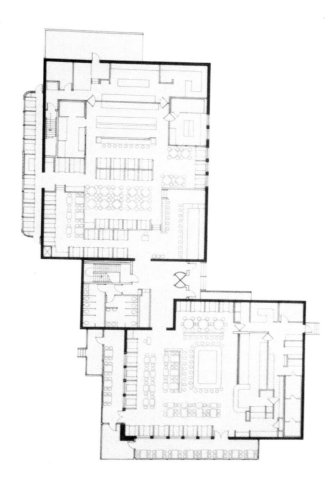

Red vinyl booths with metal coat racks, and glazed concrete walls are featured in the diner car area.

CHAPTER
8

Seafood and Ocean Theme Restaurants

Along with regular exercise, eating nutritiously has become a major part of many lifestyles in the 1980s. Light eating, which is especially recommended by doctors and nutritional experts to enjoy a healthy life, is becoming the practice of many restaurant-goers. Thus salad bars and light cuisine, once thought to be passing trends, have become solid staples in today's restaurant.

The latest, most exciting food to join the ranks of the health-conscious is seafood. Diners are enjoying it for its good nutrition, high protein, low cholesterol, and—best of all—great taste. This nutritional trend has boosted tremendously the patronage of seafood restaurants. As a result, there also has been a dramatic increase in the variety of fish and shellfish available in today's market. Stimulated by both customer appetite and culinary imagination, seafood menus have broadened to accommodate the growing number of enticing entries. Not long ago, most customers were familiar only with Dover sole (imported from England) or oysters (imported from France). Today, more and more diners prefer domestic seafood for reasons of variety, abundance, relatively low price, and proximity, which ensures freshness. Pompano from Florida, red snapper from South Carolina, and mussels from

Maine all enjoy current popularity among seafood lovers.

Restaurateurs have benefited from the seafood trend, as well. Flexibility to change seafood specials in their menus allows them to exploit whatever is available in the market. This ensures freshness, encourages innovative cooking, and provides customers with varied food choices.

Complementing the fresh, new appeal of seafood in the 1980s are the innovative design trends demonstrated by the restaurants presented in this chapter. Typical nautical theme paraphernalia—lobster traps, fishnetting, shells, heavy dark wood—is downplayed in favor of more subtler nautical themes, and lighter-colored, more contemporary interiors.

At the Seafood Shanty, the sleek, upscale atmosphere of a luxury cruise liner is created through elements such as riveted metal ceilings; white-painted handrails; a roll of sailcloth over the bar; wooden floors with tile trim; striped, angled smoke stacks; and mirrored portholes. The main dining room, too, reflects the grand oceanliner style, with light domes in the ceiling, back-lit carved mirrors, and elegant astrological charts.

Casola's Fish House sports an opaque, gray-stained, contemporary exterior. Inside, the view to the harbor has been expanded through the installation of floor-to-ceiling windows. Woodwork is painted an opaque off-white, or is sandblasted and left its natural shade. A bleached oak bar with nautical-flavored light fixtures, natural oak butcher-block tables, and light-colored wooden chairs create a relaxed seaside atmosphere.

Legal Sea Foods is divided into three main areas—a cafe, a restaurant, and a retail fish market. In the market section, fish are displayed in glass and white-porcelain cases, while the blue-and-white striped awnings, outdoor patio furniture, blue and white oilcloth-covered tables, and traditional wood slat benches of the cafe create an open, breezy quality. The mahogany and tile of the floors can withstand the eroding effects of salt water.

The painted brick, warm woods, and muted colors of Shaw's Blue Crab imitate the atmosphere of an urban East Coast crab house around World War II. The placement of the restaurant, partially overhanging a pond, gives it a wharflike appearance.

Dock's on the Upper West Side of Manhattan, is designed to look as if it has "grown up" in its location. Elements typically found in neighborhood restaurants are found here, including the straight bar with its back-mirrored display, blackboards featuring daily specials, and period promotion posters.

In Hemenway's, a 58-foot sepia-tone mural depicts Providence's waterfront 100 years ago. Platforms, seating arrangements, and low partitions are used to break up the large space. Custom lighting, neon, and ceiling fans provide a vertical layering effect.

There will always be a few who believe that French or English seafood is the best that money can buy, but the contemporary, health-conscious diner is part of an upscale market that enjoys the adventure of discovering new and exciting *domestic* seafood specialties. This sense of adventure and sensible eating style may or may not be here to stay, but the spirited seafood restaurant designs presented here seem to indicate smooth sailing ahead.

CASOLA'S
FISH HOUSE

Project Location: Marina del Rey, California
Interior Designers and Architects: Charlie Sparks (*principal-in-charge*),
Bob Felten (*project manager*),
Schafer Associates, Inc.; and
Stevie Bannister (*principal-in-charge*),
Bruce Marteney (*project manager*),
Andrea Diaz (*color and materials*),
Schafer Associates West, Inc.
General Contractor: Jack Willingham,
Willingham/Wilson

As a seafood restaurant, Casola's Fish House originally used a Spanish galleon theme design. The interior's dark wood and dim lights gave the space a heavy, dark atmosphere. The exterior was covered with weathered boards and needed drastic repairs.

An opaque grey stain and lighter trim has created a contemporary look for the exterior. The remodeling of the interior capitalizes on the exceptional harbor view. To brighten the interior of the restaurant, the existing windows and walls on the harbor-view side have been replaced with floor-to-ceiling windows, maximizing the view. Opaque off-white paint has been used on existing panels. Other wood surfaces have been sandblasted and left with their natural color.

Light wood floors at the bar/raw bar area and new carpeting in the main dining areas help create a relaxed atmosphere. Lighting is provided by pendant-hung brass fixtures with a nautical design. The bowed wooden floor of the entrance has been changed to tile flooring and the bowed wooden beams have been replaced by grooved wood painted off-white. Doors are wood with glass insets.

The bar is made of bleached oak with a marble armrest, and a brass rack is mounted overhead.

Carved glass panels, natural oak butcher-block tables, and light wood chairs used throughout the restaurant contribute to the contemporary look.

*New carpeting in the main dining area ◊
contributes to the relaxed atmosphere.*

Shown is one of the three small private-party rooms enclosed by rich draperies.

Floor-to-ceiling windows have been installed to brighten the space and provide an unobstructed view of the harbor. Woodwork is either painted opaque off-white or sandblasted and left natural.

The tile and light wooden floors create a casual atmosphere at the bar. Shining brass and blue accents add crisp interest.

SHAW'S BLUE CRAB

Project Location: Deerfield, Illinois

Client: Lettuce Entertain You Enterprises

Interior and Lighting Designer, and
Architect: Bill Aumiller, Aumiller Youngquist,
P.C.

Contractor: Capitol Construction

Engineering: Diverisifed Engineering Service, Inc.

Photography: Mark Ballogg, Steincamp-Ballogg
Photography

Local zoning ordinances allowed only one building on the selected site for Ed Debevic's Short Orders Deluxe and Shaw's Blue Crab. The main problem posed by housing the two different restaurants in one place was resolved by providing separate yet harmonious identities to the restaurants, both on the exterior and in the common lobby. (See Chapter 5, The New American Diner, for Ed Debevic's Short Orders Deluxe.)

Strong exterior identities through the use of color, shape, and design were sought because zoning ordinances restricted exterior signage.

Consequently, banding in turquoise-green for Ed Debevic's and deep red for Shaw's Blue Crab runs along the edges of the building, which is of neutral-colored glazed concrete block.

The look of Shaw's Blue Crab is rooted in the past—specifically, the World War II era. Its painted brick, warm woods, and muted colors exude memorable qualities common to East Coast urban crab houses of that time. An existing pond on the site allowed the designer to extend the restaurant's dining area over the water to create a wharf-like feel and appearance.

Warm woods and muted colors are used throughout. Shown is an overall view which includes the bar, mural and antique light fixtures.

LEGAL SEA FOODS

Project Location: Burlington Mall, Burlington, Massachusetts

Client: Legal Sea Food Restaurants, Inc.

Interior Designers: Peter Niemietz, Blase Gallo, Morris Nathanson, (*project designers*), Morris Nathanson Design, Inc.

Photographer: Warren Jagger

The first suburban location for Legal Sea Foods is in Burlington, Massachusetts. With this new move, the designers felt that the now famous "fish market" prototype design of the five urban locations would not work. Suburban Massachusetts demanded a more upscaled and relaxed atmosphere, more style, less marketplace. The major challenge to the designers was to bring this change into the design while retaining the company's identity.

The entrance to the restaurant was designed as typically "storefront" to maintain the establishment's identity with Legal Sea Foods' fish market origins. Cobalt blue and creme matte finish tiles also provide a lively graphic reference to the original fish market imagery.

The long, linear shape of the restaurant is broken up by several partitioned dining areas, while upturned halogen lights accent the vertical by highlighting the dramatic arches and vaulted ceilings. Nautically themed artwork promotes a seafaring atmosphere. Mahogany paneling and black painted chairs with tapestry contrast with the cream painted walls and with the contemporary architecture to create a pleasing blend of the new and the old New England.

The nautical atmosphere is embodied in subtle details: brass rails, nautically themed artwork mounted on the walls, and rich mahogany. The restaurant seats 210 diners in several varied partitioned areas.

DOCK'S

Project Location: New York, New York
Client: 2427-2429 Seafood Restaurant, Inc.
Interior Designers: Peter Niemitz, Blase Gallo, Morris Nathanson, (*project designers*), Morris Nathanson Design, Inc.
Photographer: Warren Jagger

The client requested a design for Dock's that would create the impression that the restaurant had "grown up" in its Upper West Side Manhattan location. The neighborhood-style restaurant is casual and owner-managed, its active bar coexisting side by side with the more sophisticated environment of its dining room.

Humble, unpretentious materials are used, such as glazed wall tile, beaded wood, classic black painted chairs, painted walls, ceramic mosaic floors, and original Holophane glass light fixtures. Typical neighborhood-style elements, such as the straight bar with its mirrored back bar display, blackboards featuring the daily specials, trophy-mounted fish, and period promotion posters, enhance the familiar atmosphere.

The functional aspects of the restaurant are the result of the period when the owner cooked for friends and family. From his own kitchen, he had a clear view of the dining room, which gave a "special order" feeling to the service. This personalized practicality was transferred to his restaurant's design.

The entire project was completed within a budget of $600,000.

"Humble" materials are used, such as beaded wood, classic black painted chairs, painted walls, ceramic mosaic bloors, and original holophane glass light fixtures.

SEAFOOD SHANTY

Project Location: Langhorne, Pennsylvania

Client: Joseph C. Gentile, (*president*), Seafood Shanty Restaurant, Inc.

Interior Designer: Robert J. DiLeonardo, DiLeonardo International

Architect: William E. Gray, A.I.A., DiLeonardo International

Photographer: Warren Jagger, Warren Jagger Photography

When the Seafood Shanty restaurant chain sought to attract upscale clientele, a new image and design concept was formulated, based on recreating the atmosphere of a sleek luxury liner. The sleek, contemporary styling begins with the exterior, which is highlighted by a red, white, and blue stripe, bands of blue neon, and a 40-foot mast encircled with a neon band. Illumination is provided by wallwashers.

The interior has a promenade deck with wood flooring and tile trim, riveted metal ceilings, white-painted steel handrails, and a continuous multi-bulb light strip that leads patrons to the different dining spaces. The bar overlooks the promenade deck and a roll of sailcloth above the bar enhances the cruise liner ambiance.

Multi-levels, painted steel railings, and uplit carved glass define three dining areas: the Upper Deck, characterized by huge striped smokestacks; the Starboard Deck with mirrored portholes; and the sunken Main Deck with a 12-foot by 12-foot skylight. The skylight is equipped with a motorized canvas shade that can be closed to diffuse the sun during the day or opened at night for dining under the stars.

Through the use of fine materials—wood, colorful tile accents, riveted steel—and refined nautical elements—portholes, painted railings—the feel of a luxury liner has been established.

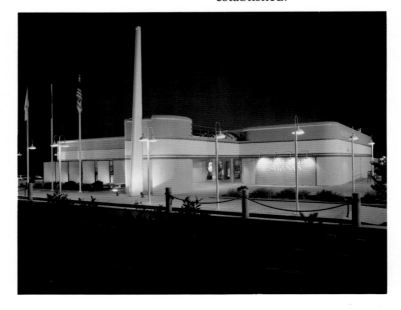

A new image for the Seafood Shanty ◊ chain has been established. It revolves around the kinds of recreation and the elegant environment found on board a luxury liner.

The luxury liner theme is carried through in the striped stacks of "The Upper Deck," one of the restaurant's three dining areas.

"The Salon" is the largest room in the restaurant, highlighted by indirectly lit ceiling domes.

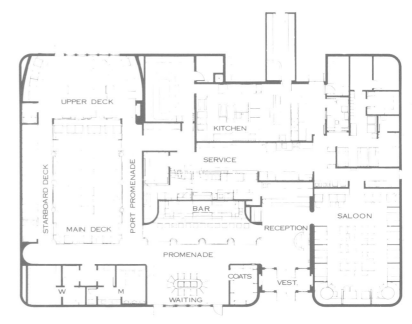

The roll of blue sailcloth over the bar enhances the nautical theme. The bar overlooks the promenade deck.

The promenade deck has polished wooden floors trimmed with tile, riveted metal ceilings, white painted handrails, and multi-bulb light strips.

HEMENWAY'S

Project Location: Providence, Rhode Island
Client: Phelps-Grace Company, Inc.
Interior Designers: Peter Niemitz, Blase Gallo, Morris Nathanson, (*project designers*), Morris Nathanson Design, Inc.
Photographer: Warren Jagger

Hemenway's is located on the street level of a newly built first-class office tower near the river in downtown Providence. The space has full-height glazing on three sides and a 20-foot ceiling. To take full advantage of the cityscape views, the bar is raised 28 inches and placed centrally. The floor plan and ceiling layout give attention to column locations and the building's structural grid pattern, and partitions, millwork, and proportions of the restaurant's interior directly reflect the architectural modules of the building.

The seafood bar and grill reflect a sense of tradition, quality, and permanence. The large area is broken up by the use of platforms, seating arrangements, and low partitions. A vertical layering effect is created through raised areas, custom lighting, neon, and ceiling fans.

The 58-foot mural dominates the space and depicts the city's waterfront one hundred years ago.

Indexes

Interior Designers

Interior Design Firms

Lighting Designers

Aumiller, Bill, **216, 230**
Bernstein, Steve, **134**
Billington, Ken, **37, 46**
Ceglic, Jack, **94**
Cline, Carroll, **72**
Kurtin-Cole, Jill & Rikki Dallow, **110**
Culver, Carol, **212**
Consolidated Edification, **56**
Domingo Gonzalez Design, **173**
Dorf, Martin E., **125, 136**
Elias, Brad, **81, 112, 127, 130, 138**
Fisher, Jules & Paul Marantz, **75**
Gainer, Celeste, **33**
Gensler & Assoc., Architects, **181**
Wheel Gersztoff Friedman Assoc., **105**
Marantz, Paul of Fisher/Marantz, **26**
Maxcy, Donald, **60**
Payne, Michael A.S.I.D., **50**
Peterson, Steven & B. Littenberg, **52**
Sapinsley, Patricia, **90**
Swearingen, Bill, **198**
Terrail, Patrick A., **210**
Tubbs, Harold E.,

Contractors

Buckeye Construction, **22**
Capitol Construction, **153, 216, 230**
David Elliot Construction, **33**
DAW Incorporated, **181**
Illig Construction Company, **148**
Mark Klinzman Construction, **39**
Mayo Construction Co., **52**
Morse Diesel Inc., **105**
Willingham, Jack, **206, 224**

Electrical Engineers

Angeles Electric, **22**
Robins Engineering, **26**

Mechanical Engineers

CCI Mechanical, **181**
Diversified Engineering Svcs., **216, 230**
G & C Consulting Engineers, **153**
Robins Engineering, **26**
Weiskopf & Pickworth, **105**
Yu, Bong P.C., **52**

Architects

Abrams, Milliken & Kent, **212**
Aumiller, Bill J., **153, 216, 230**
Barrable, Pauline, **117**
Bogdanow, Larry & Warren, Ashworth, Bonneville Architects, **181**
Brown, Day, Mullins, Dierdorf, Inc., **100**

Photographers

Abraham, Russell, **60**
Ballogg, Mark, **153, 216, 230**
Desimone, Mark, **72**
Duhamel, Francois, **210**
Eifert, Daniel, **33**
Frizzell, Charles, **212**
Glomb, David, **22**
Hoyt, Wolfgang, **75, 105**
Jagger, Warren, **66, 117, 143, 158, 162, 184, 232, 236, 240, 246**
Katz, Ken, **90**
Laine, Roland & Dan Lucente, **196**
Margonelli, Peter, **52**
McGrath, Norman, **37**
Milroy, Mark & McAleer, Mary, **46, 206**
Murphy, Gregory, **100**
Naar, Jon, **26**
Naideau, Harold, **94**
Nilsson, Phillip, **50**
Paige, Peter, **81, 112, 130, 138**
Peery, Gordon, **181**
Rohde, Mark & Ed Riddell, **39**
Ross, Mark, **173**

Artists